Women in Charge

Why do women start their own businesses? Is it solely because they are searching for financial success, or for other reasons? On the basis of detailed interviews with a number of women who have started their own businesses, this book, first published in 1985, reveals the significance of factors that are directly related to women's experiences at home, at work, and in the wider society.

The author's analysis shows how business start-up enables many women, but not all, to achieve forms of economic and social independence that they would not otherwise enjoy. Further, they illustrate ways in which business proprietorship has a wide variety of effects upon individuals, and upon their personal relationships and life styles. They refute the notion of a single entrepreneurial experience and argue that the causes and consequences of business start-up are highly conditioned by the extent to which women are committed to traditionally prescribed roles and to profitability.

The findings of this book will have important implications for the formulation of small business policies. It will also be of particular value to those interested in women's studies and small business management.

Women in Charge

The Experiences of Female Entrepreneurs

Robert Goffee

and

Richard Scase

Routledge
Taylor & Francis Group

First published in 1985
by George Allen & Unwin Ltd.

This edition first published in 2015 by Routledge
2 Park Square, Milton Park, Abingdon, Oxon, OX14 4RN
and by Routledge
711 Third Avenue, New York, NY 10017

Routledge is an imprint of the Taylor & Francis Group, an informa business

Publisher's Note
The publisher has gone to great lengths to ensure the quality of this
reprint but points out that some imperfections in the original copies may
be apparent.

Disclaimer
The publisher has made every effort to trace copyright holders and
welcomes correspondence from those they have been unable to contact.

A Library of Congress record exists under LC control number: 84024449

ISBN 13: 978-1-138-89810-3 (hbk)
ISBN 13: 978-1-315-70875-1 (ebk)

Women in Charge

The Experiences of Female Entrepreneurs

Robert Goffee and Richard Scase

London
GEORGE ALLEN & UNWIN
Boston   Sydney

George Allen & Unwin (Publishers) Ltd,
40 Museum Street, London WC1A 1LU, UK

George Allen & Unwin (Publishers) Ltd,
Park Lane, Hemel Hempstead, Herts HP2 4TE, UK

Allen & Unwin, Inc.,
Fifty Cross Street, Winchester, Mass. 01890, USA

George Allen & Unwin Australia Pty Ltd,
8 Napier Street, North Sydney, NSW 2060, Australia

First published in 1985

British Library Cataloguing in Publication Data

Goffee, Robert
  Women in charge: the experiences of female entrepreneurs.
1. Women in business 2. Women-owned business enterprises
I. Title II. Scase, Richard
305.4'3338   HQ1233
ISBN 0–04–301189–6
ISBN 0–04–301190–X Pbk

Library of Congress Cataloging in Publication Data

Goffee, Robert
  Women in charge.
Bibliography: p.
Includes index.
1. Women-owned business enterprises – Great Britain. 2. Entrepreneur.
3. Women in business. 4. Small business – Great Britain. I. Scase, Richard.
II. Title.
HD2346.G7G63   1985   338'.04'088042   84–24449
ISBN 0–04–301189–6 (alk. paper)
ISBN 0–04–301190–X (pbk.: alk. paper)

Set in 11 on 12 point Garamond by
Phoenix Photosetting, Chatham, Kent
and printed in Great Britain by
Hazell Watson and Viney Limited,
Member of the BPCC Group, Aylesbury, Bucks

Contents

Contents

Preface

In this book we describe the experiences of a number of women who have started their own businesses. More specifically, we assess how far this has enabled them to be successful in a society in which there are widespread gender inequalities. This is the third of our books on business owners, the earlier of which discussed the experiences of men (Scase and Goffee, 1980a, 1982).

We are grateful to the Economic and Social Research Council and to the Nuffield Foundation for the funding of the research; to Mina Bowater and Maxine Pollock for helping us with many of the interviews; and to Barbara Holland, Vicky Marriott and Sue Steele for typing the various drafts of this book. But, above all, we are indebted to all those women who so willingly discussed their business and personal lives with us. This book is for them.

R.G.
R.S.

The Emerging Trends

1

Women and Proprietorship in the 1980s

Over recent years the position of women in the economy has attracted considerable attention (Amsden, ed., 1980; West, ed., 1982; Joseph, 1983). In many ways this reflects their growing participation in the labour market and the success of the women's movement in focusing attention upon gender-related inequalities. But despite recent debates, many issues remain unexplored. The actual working experiences of women, for example, have not been systematically and thoroughly investigated although a number of studies have been recently undertaken (McNally, 1979; Pollert, 1981; Cavendish, 1982; Coyle, 1984). Discussions of women's subordination, moreover, have often been theoretically orientated and unsubstantiated by detailed empirical inquiry. At the same time, an emphasis upon working women as employees has led to the neglect of those who are employers and who run their own businesses. This book is intended to help redress this imbalance.

The neglect of women in studies of the workplace is well illustrated in the contents of many standard texts on industrial behaviour (Miller and Form, 1964; Burns, ed., 1969; Fox, 1971). In most cases, women are either totally excluded from consideration or they are assumed to behave in much the same way as men. The findings of industrial social research are almost entirely based upon the study of men within male-dominated industries and occupations and these have then provided the information upon which industrial studies have developed as academic and applied disciplines. Thus, it is investigations of men in industries such as coal mining (Dennis, Henriques and Slaughter, 1969), shipbuilding (Brown *et al.*, 1972), printing (Cannon, 1967) and car assembly (Goldthorpe *et al.*, 1968) which provide the 'hard data' for general theories about all workers' attitudes and behaviour. These observations, furthermore, have then often been related to discussions of family relationships, leisure patterns and life-styles (Dennis, Henriques and Slaughter, 1969, Goldthorpe *et al.*, 1968). As a result, women – both inside and outside paid employment – appear as highly marginal figures. If women have been studied at work it has been either explicitly stated or implicitly assumed – certainly until quite recently – that their attitudes and behaviour differ little from men. Indeed, this view is evident from the very beginnings of industrial social research, the classic example of which is the much-quoted Hawthorne Investigation conducted in the United States during the 1930s (Roethlisberger and Dickson, 1939). In this study many of the work teams were women but the researchers gave little consideration to the possibility that employees' gender could affect their attitudes to work, social relationships and workplace behaviour. As Brown has suggested in his discussion of key themes within industrial sociology,

> the body of research which attempts to explore the relationship between such factors as supervision, participation, informal social groups, and productivity, morale and acceptance of change, does not really consider, though it does report, the sex of the workers who were the subjects of the investigations as being any sort of limitation on the generality of the conclusions . . .
>
> My argument . . . is not that men are so different that no generalisations, or accounts of genetic social processes in industrial situations, can possibly be true for both sexes; rather that the possible significance of the different social situations which men and women are in, by virtue of their gender, both within and outside the factory (and these can change), must always be considered in evaluating any research which it is argued has general implications. (1976, p. 26)

It is only recently that researchers, and particularly feminists, have begun to conduct studies of the experiences of women as these are shaped by male-dominated control structures within industrial organizations and, outside of work, by the general institutions and values of capitalism (Purcell, 1979; Herzog, 1980; Wajcman, 1983). These offer an empirical or factual corrective to the more abstract themes which have characterized many Marxist debates about the position of women in capitalist society. Women as employees, then, after much neglect are now attracting the attention of social researchers.

However, little is known of the experiences of women as employers and as owner-managers of business enterprises. While anthropologists have studied the position of women traders in non-industrialized countries (Caplan, ed., 1978) there has been an almost complete neglect of the contribution that women make to the formation and growth of businesses, particularly those of a small-scale, in the advanced capitalist societies (see Chapter 2). In view of the importance of small businesses as providers of employment, goods and services in the Western economies of the 1980s, this is a significant omission; particularly since women contribute to the process of business formation and growth in at least two major ways.

First, married women often provide a variety of hidden and unpaid services to their husbands' businesses during the crucial start-up period. As we have discussed elsewhere, without this largely unrecognized contribution many male-owned enterprises would not get off the ground (Scase and Goffee, 1980a, 1980b, 1982). Self-employed men, for instance, can be heavily dependent upon their wives' efforts for undertaking a wide range of clerical and administrative duties. Accordingly, these married women are often forced to give up their paid jobs and to abandon their careers in order to underwrite the efforts of their 'self-made' husbands. Economically, socially and psychologically, therefore, the wives of small businessmen are often subordinated to the needs of their husbands. Further, because these men devote such a high proportion of their time and energy to their businesses, their wives are often compelled to cope single-handedly with domestic chores, including those of child-rearing and household budgeting. This is often with limited financial resources since these, too, may be stretched by the start-up requirements of the business. Unfortunately, there is little detailed information about the specific dynamics involved in these processes. There are, for example, no systematic data on the nature of entrepreneurial families, the formation of conjugal roles, and the ways in which business formation and growth are shaped by negotiations between husbands and wives. There is even less information on the attitudes and behaviour of business owners' wives and the ways in which they respond to their unpaid work and domestic roles. The entrepreneurial family, then, may be considered to be of considerable interest if only because, as a unit of economic production, it possesses features which are quite distinct from the 'normal' family which primarily functions as a unit of consumption.

There is, however, a second and more direct way in which women contribute to the formation and growth of small businesses; that is, by starting their own enterprises. But, again, little is known about the processes involved (Goffee and Scase, 1982b, 1983a, 1983c; Goffee, Scase and Pollack, 1982). Feminists, for instance, have shown little interest, if only because of a belief that business ownership sustains an economic system which maintains the subordination of women by men. Accordingly, there has been hardly any discussion of proprietorship as a possible avenue whereby women can overcome their subordination within the family, the workplace and in society as a whole. Generally, feminists argue that the personal benefits which can be derived from proprietorship do not improve the general conditions experienced by most women. Many argue that individual strategies of 'self-determination' through proprietorship are contrary to many of the central ideals of sisterhood and do not offer a realistic alternative to collective action (Novarra, 1980). Consequently, because of the widespread acceptance of this argument the socio-economic processes associated with female proprietorship have been neglected. How, for instance, do specifically gender-related experiences affect women who start their own businesses? This is an important question if only because the economic conditions of the 1980s may be leading to an increase in the number of women embarking upon proprietorial careers. If there are a number of factors contributing to this trend, there would seem to be three which are of particular importance: those of high unemployment, job dissatisfaction and the development of new technology.

With high levels of long-term unemployment in various 'female' sectors of the economy (Sinfield, 1981; West, ed., 1982), proprietorship is becoming an important means of employment for many women. Those who are economically marginalized because of the lack of opportunities for paid employment may have no option but to start their own businesses as a source of earnings (Goffee and Scase, 1983a). But even those who are gainfully employed may be increasingly attracted to entrepreneurship because of the experience of various forms of workplace deprivation. Because of their concentration in lowly skilled and low-paid occupations, a considerable proportion of women have little opportunity for meaningful job satisfaction (Wainwright, 1978; Webb, 1982). Even the small minority of those who are engaged in more economically and psychologically rewarding managerial and professional occupations are likely to encounter gender-related prejudices which can heighten their levels of stress and limit their career prospects (Hennig and Jardim, 1979; Silverstone and Ward, eds, 1980; Cooper and Davidson, 1982). If, then, as various studies have shown, a dissatisfaction with paid employment can often encourage men to start their own businesses (MacKenzie, 1973; Bechhofer *et al.*, 1974b; Scase and Goffee, 1980a) the office and shopfloor experiences of women are likely to have similar effects (Goffee and Scase, 1982b). Finally, as recent experience in the United States suggests, the development of new micro-electronic technology of the sort that can be used in the home is offering new possibilities for the formation of small businesses among both men and women (see Chapter 2). With the relevant skills, many women are now able to trade at home as the self-employed providers of a wide range of administrative, financial and technical services.

In the 1980s, then, an increasing number of women are likely to start their own businesses (Boissevain, 1980; US Small Business Administration, 1982). Because many will have been in either full-time or part-time paid employment, they will have often acquired skills which are useful for business start-up. In the service sector, for example, where most women are employed, practical skills can be more important for starting a small business than access to financial resources (Goffee and Scase, 1982b, 1983b). A very large proportion of small firms in the service sector begin on a very limited scale, often utilizing domestic premises and the proprietors' own skills and the only finance required for such ventures is obtained from personal savings (Scase and Goffee, 1980a). Such a pattern of small business start-up has been encouraged by the growth of the 'informal' economy which during the economic recession of the past decade has provided a context within which women – as well as men – can, on a limited scale, 'experiment' with business proprietorship (Pahl, 1980). In Britain, the United States and in several other industrial countries, there has been a tendency to substitute the 'informal', the 'household' and the 'cash' production of goods and services for those produced within the 'formal' economy (Gershuny, 1978). It seems reasonable to expect, therefore, that as unemployment among women continues to grow, many will increasingly search for ways of earning a means of living through these 'informal' and 'cash' patterns of trading. This, in turn, can provide a springboard for legitimate business start-up and the longer-term acquisition of entrepreneurial talents. In these ways, then, more and more women are likely to start their own businesses, even though they are likely to remain a very small minority of all women. Furthermore, it must be emphasized that a large number of self-employed women are only formally economically 'independent'; in reality they can be lowly paid and easily expendable 'out' or 'home' workers who provide subcontracting services for larger companies (Cragg and Dawson, 1981; Allen, 1983). Even so, there are a number of trends to suggest that women are more likely to start their own independent businesses now than in the past.

In this book we study the experiences of these women: the benefits they obtain and the difficulties they encounter. More particularly, we are interested in the extent to which women are able to overcome experiences of subordination through business proprietorship. On the basis of in-depth interviews with a number of women business owners, we investigate their motives and the consequent experiences of entrepreneurship. It seems reasonable to assume that although many women are similar to men in their expectations of the rewards to be derived from small business ownership, they will face distinctively gender-related problems. The next chapter describes the position of women in the labour market in general, in order to provide a context within which the incidence and pattern of female proprietorship may be more fully explored.

2

Women, the Economy and Avenues for Business Start-Up

One of the more striking features of the postwar British economy has been the increasing proportion of women in paid employment (Webb, 1982). Most, however, have been recruited into a limited range of occupations, and gender divisions within the labour market have been reinforced by their concentration in light industrial and service-sector jobs (Hakim, 1979). In this chapter, we discuss the factors which account for the increased employment of women and describe their distribution in the labour market. As we shall show, the pattern of self-employment and female proprietorship tends to reflect the character and spread of female employment within the economy as a whole.

Approximately 40 per cent of the labour force in Britain today are women. The postwar increase mainly reflects a considerable growth in the number of married women who go out to work. Whereas only one in ten were working in Britain in 1931, there were one in five by 1951 and one in two by the mid-1970s (Department of Employment, 1975a). A similar trend is evident in other countries. In the United States, for example, the proportion of married women in employment grew from less than 25 per cent in 1950 to 43 per cent by the late 1970s (Manpower Report, 1977). There seems to be at least four major factors which account for this trend. First, *structural* processes relating to changes in systems of large-scale production and administration have created routine and semi-skilled white-collar and manual occupations which have been filled to a large extent by women (Braverman, 1974). They have been increasingly employed to perform lesser-skilled clerical tasks and, as West points out, to 'assemble, pack or sell things – clothes, textiles, food, drink – "consumer goods" once provided within the home' (1982, p. 3). In addition, female wage labour is responsible for providing a variety of personal services

such as 'cleaning, washing, and teaching and health care too, for
organisations rather than private individuals' (West, 1982, p. 3).
In fact, it has even been argued that a major motive underlying the
implementation of new technological processes within large-scale
administrative and productive systems has been to destroy skilled
jobs so that relatively expensive and highly trained male workers
can be replaced by cheaper, semi-skilled female operatives (Beechey, 1982). Secondly, a number of *demographic* changes have
enabled more women to take up full-time paid employment; they
now marry earlier, live to an older age and have fewer children
within a shorter and earlier period of their lives (Joseph, 1983).
This has allowed a larger number of women to seek employment
when family obligations have receded during early middle age.
Thirdly, there has been a restructuring of *psychological* expectations
which has led many women to search for work-related rather than
marriage-based self-identities. A major factor accounting for this
has been the growing extent to which women have acquired
qualifications within higher educational institutions (Wilkin,
1982; Davidson and Cooper, 1983b). Thus, for many of these
women careers at work rather than marriage are seen to offer a more
important route for self-fulfilment. Finally, within the context of
recession, the need to maintain living standards seems to be an
important *economic* reason why many women seek paid employment.
Again, as West points out, 'it is not simply that aspirations may
have risen, but rather that it is the income of wives which keeps
many families above the poverty line' (1982, p. 3). The importance of the earnings of married women for family living standards
is particularly significant in the context of long-term high unemployment. A recent survey found that approximately one-half of all
employed married women in Britain were working because they
'really need the money' (Dunnell, 1979, p. 31). Similarly, a
survey of EEC countries suggested that a substantial proportion of
married women employees were at work because of either 'necessity' or 'insufficient salary of the spouse' (Eurostat, 1981, table 91).
Despite an increase in the number of women in paid employment,
they remain concentrated in a limited range of industries and
occupations. Further, 'even where women work alongside men,
they usually hold positions of lower responsibility and perform
tasks of a less skilled nature . . . men are the employers, managers,

top professionals, foremen and skilled workers in our society'
(Central Statistical Office, 1974, p. 16). Indeed, as a recent report
has argued, gender-based divisions within the labour market are
found in all capitalist economies:

> The pattern as far as job opportunities is concerned is fairly uniform
> throughout the Western World. The range of openings and occupa-
> tions available to women is limited, and prospects within these
> occupations are less good for women than for men. Although
> relatively few professions and occupations are specifically closed to
> women, a fairly clear distinction is drawn in the labour market of
> most countries between jobs for men and for women. Most women
> work within a limited range of occupations which employ in most
> cases largely, or only, women. (Department of Employment,
> 1975b, p. 2)

Of course, gender represents but one criterion according to which
labour-market segmentation occurs. Other divisions operate on
the basis of such factors as ethnicity, age and skill. Consequently,
many writers draw a distinction between 'primary' and 'secondary'
sectors within a 'dual' labour market (Doeringer and Piore, 1971;
Gordon, 1972). According to Barron and Norris (1976), for
example, primary-sector jobs offer higher wages, personal autonomy and responsibility, good employment conditions, security
and prospects of career advancement while secondary-sector
occupations are characterized by low pay, poor working conditions, limited career prospects, little autonomy and responsibility,
and virtually no job security. But why is it that most employed
women within Western economies are in 'secondary' occupations?
Barron and Norris explain this by reference to five factors.

First, employers are able to move women more easily from jobs
than men. Women are also more likely to change jobs and move in
and out of the labour market more frequently because of their
family and domestic responsibilities. As a result, they are generally
perceived to have a relatively weak claim on jobs. As Barron and
Norris point out,

> Women are commonly held to be more dispensable than men . . .
> because of the strength of family values – and even when a woman's
> income may be vital to family living standards, it is often said that

her 'real' place is in the home with her family and that her husband
is, or should be, the main source of income. (1976, p. 55)

In periods of economic recession, therefore, a prevailing ideology
of 'male entitlement' to scarce jobs becomes particularly pronounced and this is often used by employers to facilitate the
removal of female employees with a minimum degree of resistance.

Secondly, women constitute a clearly visible and differentiated
subordinate social group. Gender divisions are firmly established
in society and just as the subordination of women to men is taken
for granted and assumed so, too, is their exclusion from certain
economic spheres. Thus, the concentration of women in low-paid
occupations is seen as 'inevitable' because of

widespread feelings that it is not right for women to earn as much or
more than their husbands or that women should not be in positions
of authority over men at the workplace, and partly because the
sexual categorisation of jobs into men's and women's work enables
the question to be avoided: women are lower paid as a group because
their sort of work is low paid. (ibid., p. 58)

Thirdly, according to Barron and Norris, women tend to display a
low interest in training and job-related educational programmes.
This can be explained by reference to general socialization processes which emphasize the different 'qualities' required for 'men's
work' by comparison to 'women's work' and to family and domestic commitments which limit women's ability to undertake
lengthy periods of occupational training. Further, this reluctance
to obtain qualifications is a function of the extent to which women
recognize the limited career opportunities which are available to
them. Since secondary jobs are predominantly unskilled and
employers are unwilling or unable to invest in training, women,
together with other minority groups, are seen to be an 'appropriate' source of cheap labour.

Fourthly, Barron and Norris argue that women often place a
lower value on the monetary rewards of employment than men.
However, as these authors emphasize, their less economistic ori-
entation does not mean that they actually have 'more limited
financial needs in any objective sense, nor can this aspect of

women's approach to work be dissociated from the fact that expectations held by women may be limited by the relatively low pay of the jobs available to them'. (ibid., p. 63)

Finally, women are less likely to engage in work-based collective action which could help to reduce their market vulnerability. Their concentration in less-secure, lower-paid, part-time occupations with high levels of turnover limits the effectiveness of union organization and leads to a 'low level of interest by many women in careerism (work as a life-time prospect) or high pay' and this, in turn, 'reduces the need, in the eyes of many women, for solidaristic activity' (ibid., p. 64). This problem is further exaggerated by the dominance of men within the established union movement, even within those unions where female membership is high.

Women, then, constitute a major element of the secondary labour force within all Western capitalist economies. Indeed, other divisions, based upon such factors as ethnicity, race and skill tend to reinforce rather than undermine deep-rooted gender inequalities (Day, 1982). The subordinate position of Asian women in Britain, for example, is particularly pronounced. Indeed, Marxist theorists, in discussing the dispensability of women within the labour market, often view them as a 'reserve army' which can be brought into, or thrown out of, employment according to the dictates of large-scale corporations (Braverman, 1974; Bruegel, 1982). According to such writers, this 'flexibility' enables employers to respond swiftly to technological change and to market fluctuations while, at the same time, women as a 'surplus reservoir' of labour serve to depress general wage levels and thereby increase the level of worker exploitation. Although women cannot be regarded as the only industrial reserve army – migrants, immigrants and school-leavers often fulfil a similar function – they are, nevertheless, as Oakley points out, 'obvious candidates because of the ease with which they can be made, or seem, to "disappear" back into the family – a structure that rests on the assumption (though often not the reality) of male support' (1982, p. 136). Women, then, are an important source of surplus labour during periods of economic expansion which can be more easily disposed of during periods of recession. Wainright describes their vulnerability in the following terms:

Given the increasingly lengthy periods of recession which periodically and unpredictably affect the capitalist economy, the sexual division of labour provides a unique advantage to capitalism. No other group is so well situated from capital's point of view. The sexual division of labour and the ideology that justifies it ensures that women are not dependent for this subsistence on wage labour. Among workers in a capitalist society they are unique in having access to a means, or a partial means, of a livelihood on the basis of social relations other than economic exchange relations. It is almost as if capitalism was able to preserve a rural economy for workers to return to, and yet make use of them whenever necessary (1978, p. 195).

Many of these arguments are confirmed by the employment data for Britain. These show a clear separation between 'men's and women's work' and a concentration of the latter within specific industrial sectors. As Oakley points out:

More than half of employed women in Britain work in three service industries: the distributive trades (shops, mail order, warehouse) – 17 per cent; 'professional and scientific' (typists, secretaries, teachers and nurses) – 23 per cent; 'miscellaneous services' (laundries, catering, dry cleaners, launderettes) – 12 per cent. A quarter of employed women work in manufacturing industries. Of these, half are in only four industries: food and drink manufacture, clothing and footwear, textiles, and electrical engineering. (1982, p. 151)

By contrast, men are not so highly concentrated within such a limited number of industries. Even so, many industries do display a clearly defined gender profile as indicated in Table 2.1.

The industries within which women predominate are, then, insurance and banking, the distributive and retail trades, miscellaneous services, professional and scientific services, and clothing and footwear. By contrast, and not surprisingly, traditional industries of mining, shipbuilding, construction, engineering and agriculture are almost exclusively the preserve of men.

Although there are these sharp contrasts in the gender profiles of different industrial sectors, men dominate the authority structures of both 'male' and 'female' industries. In banking, for example, where a high proportion of employees are women, less than 1 per cent of all branch managers are women, while even in the female-

Table 2.1 *Industrial Distribution of Male and Female Employees in Britain, 1981*

Industrial sector	Percentage men	Percentage women
Mining and quarrying	95	5
Construction	92	8
Shipbuilding and marine engineering	91	9
Coal and petroleum products	90	10
Vehicles	89	11
Mechanical engineering	85	15
Agriculture, forestry, fishing	82	18
Transport and communication	81	19
Gas, electricity and water	79	21
Paper, printing and publishing	69	31
Electrical engineering	67	33
Food, drink and tobacco	61	39
Public administration	58	42
Textiles	55	45
Insurance, banking, finance and business services	49	51
Distributive and retail trades	47	53
Miscellaneous services	47	53
Professional and scientific services	31	69
Clothing and footwear	26	74

Source: Department of Employment (1982), table 135.

dominated clerical and retail sales occupations no more than 15 and 26 per cent of managers respectively, are women (Oakley, 1982, tables 7.5, 7.6).

The most significant increases in women's employment over the past decades have been in their recruitment into routine clerical and unskilled manual occupations. Both sorts of jobs offer lower pay and little work satisfaction because of the growth of large-scale productive and administrative systems, the development of rigorous and impersonal forms of managerial control, and the widespread implementation of new technology (Salaman, 1979). All of these factors have 'de-humanized' the work experiences of female employees and restricted their opportunities for promotion and self-enrichment. Table 2.2 illustrates the extent to which women are confined to routine and lower-status jobs.

Table 2.2   *Occupation, Distribution of Men and Women in Britain, 1978*

Occupational group	*Women in the occupational group as percentage of women in the workforce*	*Men in the occupational group as percentage of men in the workforce*
Managerial and professional	26	32
Clerical and other non-manual	30	5
Foremen and supervisors	5	8
Skilled manual	10	32
Unskilled and semi-skilled manual	29	23
TOTAL	100	100

Source: Webb (1982), table 6.12.

Nevertheless, despite these trends, there has been an increase in the number of women entering managerial, administrative and professional occupations. Thus, Cooper and Davidson claim that during the 1970s,

> there was a 33 per cent increase in women graduates entering industrial employment; the number of women in finance and accounting rose from 14 per cent to 23 per cent in that period; in legal work from 25 per cent to 32 per cent; in personnel management from 51 per cent to 62 per cent; and in marketing, selling and buying from 28 per cent to 36 per cent. This trend has been reinforced by the increasing number of women taking university courses in management. Taking a look at the main universities running undergraduate courses in management in the U.K., the number rose from 187 in 1973 to 770 in 1977; as a proportion of all management students, the percentage increased from 12 per cent to 27 per cent; and in the three largest management departments, the increase was from roughly 10 per cent in that same period. In 1981 over 40 per cent of the total management students in the largest university management department were female. Similar upward trends are happening in the U.S. with the percentage of women enrolled in graduate business schools in 1979 being 17 per cent at

Chicago University's School of Business Administration, 25 per cent at Harvard Business School, 26 per cent at Stanford Business School, and 35 per cent at Columbia. (1982, pp. 15–17)

It does seem, therefore, that there are now more academically qualified women competing with men for higher managerial and professional occupations and that female recruitment into these jobs is increasing. Between 1971 and 1980, for instance, the percentage of female members of the Chartered Insurance Institute increased from 4 per cent to 10 per cent; the Institute of Bankers from 1 per cent to 13 per cent; and the Law Society from 3 per cent to 12 per cent (Webb, 1982, table 6.13). Nevertheless, women still predominate in the 'caring', 'semi-professions' of social work, nursing and teaching, and their numbers have continued to expand in the 'lower' professions of advertising and public relations, personnel management, journalism and publishing. Even so, they only constitute approximately one-fifth of the members of the Institute of Personnel Managers, one-quarter of the National Union of Journalists and one-tenth of the executive staff of advertising agencies (Mackie and Patullo, 1977, ch. 4). As Mackie and Patullo have argued, 'women tend to occupy the by-ways of the professions rather than the mainstream; they dominate in the back-up, services areas rather than the powerhouses' (1977, p. 91).

The pattern of female employment in Britain also tends to be found in other Western economies, irrespective of their political cultures and the strength of their respective labour movements. Both in Sweden and in the United States, for example, women are concentrated in low-status, lesser-skilled and poorly paid occupations. Such similarities are possibly surprising in view of Sweden's somewhat more influential labour movement and the extent to which unionization amongst women workers is higher. Table 2.3 provides some comparative, albeit rudimentary, data on the distribution of women between selected occupations in Britain, Sweden and the United States.

In all of the Western economies it appears that women are 'predominant in office work, the retail trade, service industries, light unskilled factory work and many para-medical jobs' (Department of Employment, 1975b, p. 2). By contrast, in every

Table 2.3   *The Proportion of Women in Selected Occupations in Britain, Sweden and the United States*

Occupation	Percentage of Women's Share		
	Sweden	United States	Britain
Secretarial and clerks	87	96	99
Nurses	97	98	91
School teachers	79	72	64
Cashiers	75	82	—
Tailors and seamstresses	94	97	99
Shop assistants	98	84	81
Cleaners	88	68	87

Source: Oppenheimer (1970), table 1; Swedish Institute (1980); Central Office of Information (1975).

Western country they are in a minority in the more highly paid and prestigious managerial and professional occupations. For example, women constitute 16 per cent of such employees in France, 17 per cent in Germany, 11 per cent in Sweden, 19 per cent in Britain and 24 per cent in the United States (Cooper and Davidson, 1982, table 1.1.).

Recent legislative attempts to break down gender-based labour market inequalities have been hindered by economic recession which, according to Hakim has promoted a climate of opinion which, 'may provide less support and encouragement for women to break down "traditional" barriers to working in typically male jobs' (1981, p. 526). Further, the marginal position of women has been reinforced by their increasing vulnerability to unemployment. The growth in the number of women registered as unemployed has been a marked feature of recent years. As Sinfield has pointed out for Britain:

> Many more women are now out of work and their unemployment is lasting longer. In summer 1980 there were twice as many women who had been out of work for the whole of the first six months of the year as were out of work at all ten years ago. The rapid increase in the numbers of women out of work has been one of the most dramatic changes in unemployment during the last decade. From very low levels in the 1950s and 1960s the number of women registered unemployed has increased sevenfold since 1970, coupled with a doubling of unemployment amongst men. (1981, p. 83)

These figures, however, underestimate the real level of female unemployment since many women who are out of work and seeking paid work fail to officially register and so do not appear in government unemployment statistics. Indeed, it has been calculated that as many as 43 per cent of unemployed married women in Britain in 1980 were not formally registered as such (Sinfield, 1981). The vulnerability of women to unemployment is directly related to their predominant position within the secondary sector of the labour market and to a specific feature of their employment; namely, their concentration in part-time jobs. Over 40 per cent of all employed women in Britain are engaged on a part-time basis and, as Bruegel argues:

> It is part-time workers who have been made to bear the brunt of the decline in employment. The pattern in electrical engineering shows this up particularly well. Between 1974 and 1977, 38,000 unskilled and semi-skilled jobs were lost; 18,000 of these were part-time jobs done by women. This represents a 40 per cent decline for part-time women workers, compared to a 5 per cent job loss among men. The 'selection' of women for redundancy . . . highlights the function of part-time employment in a capitalist economy. Whenever short-term fluctuations in demand for labour are expected . . . the cost of dealing with such fluctuations for the capitalist is less when women, particularly part-time women, have been employed . . . In every industry where employment declined between 1974 and 1977, the rate of decline for part-time women, exceeded that of men and full-time women. It is part-time women workers, who form an increasing proportion of women workers . . . who conform most closely to the model of women as a disposable reserve army. (1982, p. 285)

In view of these general patterns of employment, what are the implications for the incidence and distribution of female proprietorship? Certainly, it would seem that neither their marginal position within the labour market, nor their subordination at work are conducive to women obtaining the technical expertise, managerial experience and financial competence to engage in entrepreneurial ventures. It is not surprising, therefore, that there are so few women business proprietors in Britain. But it is difficult to determine their exact numbers since there are no comprehensive data on them.[1] There are, however, official statistics on women classified as 'employers', 'self-employed' and those 'working on their own account'. Unfortunately, there are major problems in interpreting these figures since it is almost impossible to distinguish between those who may be genuinely regarded as independent business proprietors and those who, classified as 'self-employed', are, in all but the legal sense, the employees and outworkers of others (Leighton, 1983). Bearing in mind these reservations it is possible to obtain a general pattern. Thus, it would appear that women who are classified as either 'employers' or 'self-employed' constitute only 4 per cent of the total female labour force (Royal Commission on Income Distribution and Wealth, 1979, table 2.11). Even so, their numbers have increased from around 300,000 in the early 1950s to over 400,000 in the 1980s (Royal Commission on Income Distribution and Wealth, 1979, table 2.11; Office of Population Censuses and Surveys, 1981). But they still only make up 20 per cent of all those officially classified as employers and the self employed (Eurostat, 1981, tables 18.1, 29).

As might be expected, the distribution of these female proprietors reflects the broader gender-based segmentation of the labour market. As Table 2.4 indicates, over three-quarters of all female employers and self-employed are to be found in the three official categories of 'sales', 'services, sports and recreation' and 'professional and technical'.

Included within these broad categories are women who own businesses providing secretarial services; proprietors of retail outlets

Table 2.4 *Occupational Distribution of Women Employers and Self-Employed in Britain, 1971*

Occupation	Percentage
Farming, forestry and fishing	9
Clothing	4
Clerical	6
Sales	40
Services, sports and recreation	26
Professional and technical	11
Others	4
Total	100

Source: Royal Commission on Income Distribution and Wealth (1979), table 2.13.

(including, for example, fashion shops, hairdressers, beauticians and dry cleaners); owners of boarding houses, hotels, restaurants and cafes, and women running contract catering and cleaning businesses. Also included are the proprietors of enterprises offering technical and professional expertise in areas such as advertising, market research, public relations, accounting, financial and insurance services; as well as the owners of publishing and literary agencies. Indeed, in terms of absolute numbers, there were 37,000 self-employed women engaged in the provision of 'professional and technical services' in Britain in 1975. During the same year there were 30,000 self-employed female hairdressers and 53,000 self-employed women were running hotels, snack bars and cafes (Royal Commission on Income Distribution and Wealth, 1979, (table 2.14). Outside the service sector there were very few women proprietors of manufacturing businesses, although a tradition of home-based craft produce is continued by self-employed women engaged in, for example, leatherwork, pottery, engraving, dressmaking and interior furnishings.

In general, the great majority of female proprietors in Britain provide less-skilled services, while a minority are engaged in highly skilled professional and technical activities. There are, however, two further features of female-owned businesses. They tend to be of recent origin and small-scale with few or no employees.[2] Both these characteristics are a reflection of their concentration within the service sector which has rapidly expanded during the postwar era (Goffee and Scase, 1982b, 1983b). Thus, with the exception of a very small number of well-known proprietors who run large businesses almost all women business owners are in charge of very small enterprises.

This, then, concludes a brief review of the position of women in the labour market. Essentially, they experience subordination within almost every sector of the economy. Does, then, entrepreneurship offer an appropriate strategy whereby women can overcome this? In the next chapter, we shall consider the various individual and collective means which are available to them.

Notes: Chapter 2

1   The lack of information on women business owners is apparent in most industrialized economies. Indeed, to our knowledge, only the United States government has attempted to systematically collect quantitative data on women proprietors. We refer to this material in Chapter 3.

2   In the Bolton Report (Committee of Inquiry on Small Firms, 1971) 96 per cent of firms in hotel and catering and the retail trades are classified as 'small'; the figure rises to 99 per cent for 'miscellaneous services'. These are popular areas for female proprietors who are more likely to be founder owners because of the tendency for businesses to be passed down to sons rather than daughters. Figures for the United States indicate that the majority of women-owned enterprises are run by founders rather than inheritors (US Department of Commerce, 1980).

3

Tackling Subordination: the Available Strategies

People respond to subordination in various ways. Indeed, there continue to be lengthy debates concerned with explaining why, in some situations, conditions of injustice and deprivation are largely accepted, while in others there is opposition and resistance (Runciman, 1966; Mann, 1973; Westergaard and Resler, 1976). Women, similarly, have responded to their subordination in ways which have varied over time and between societies. In Western countries large numbers of women seem to have become more resentful about their generally deprived circumstances. As a result, many of them are pursuing a variety of individual and collective strategies which enable them, both directly and indirectly, to combat gender-related disadvantages. It is in this sense that female entrepreneurship may be interpreted. Indeed, under capitalism – and particularly in the United States – business proprietorship has traditionally offered a means whereby individual members of deprived groups have striven to overcome conditions of subordination (Mills, 1953; Kornhauser, 1960; Light, 1972). However, this is but one possibility since individual advancement can also be pursued through occupational careers within large-scale organizations. These opportunities have increased during the postwar era and a small but increasing number of women are now engaged in various administrative, managerial and professional careers (Fogarty, Allen and Walters, 1981; Davidson and Cooper, 1983b). But, in addition to these individual means, women may also confront their subordination more collectively. The labour and women's movements, for example, offer mechanisms whereby 'women's rights' can be pursued. Despite their different traditions and ideologies both movements share, to quote J. Hunt, 'linking philosophies, one held by the women's movement of the importance of women "getting together" to discuss problems and develop confidence and activity. The other, that of the trade union organisation, lies within the organising strength of the workplace' (1982 p. 171). In this chapter, therefore, we shall consider these collective strategies as well as those of a more individual kind which are normally associated with career mobility and entre-preneurial success.

Although the labour movements of most Western countries are committed to improving the rights of women, their achievements as yet have been far from impressive. As Oakley has remarked, 'The situation of women in the trade unions in many countries, Britain and the United States included, nowhere near represents their importance in production . . . These bodies have not promoted issues of direct relevance to women' (1982, pp. 304–6). Indeed, this continuing neglect of issues that are important to women is surprising in view of their growing participation in the labour market and within many trade unions. In Britain, for example, women have been the largest source of recruitment for unions during the postwar era and by the early 1980s about one-third of all women in employment were union members (J. Hunt, 1982). Further, as Table 3.1 shows, the percentage of trade union members who are women has increased from 11 per cent in 1939 to 29 per cent in 1978.

Table 3.1   *Trade Union Membership in Britain, 1939–78*

Year	Men (000s)	Women (000s)	Total (000s)	Women as a percentage of total union membership
1939	4,116	553	4,669	11
1958	6,950	1,387	8,337	17
1968	6,959	1,767	8,726	20
1978	8,454	3,411	11,865	29

Source: J. Hunt (1982), table 9.1.

The growth of women's membership was particularly rapid during the 1960s and 1970s, when there was a considerable expansion of female employment in the public sector and an associated increase in white-collar unionism. This, as shown in Table 3.2, is reflected in the high proportion of women in a limited number of mainly white-collar trade unions.

Table 3.2   *The Increase in Women's Membership of Trade Unions in Britain,* 1968–78

Union	Actual increase in no. of women (000s)	Percentage increase in no. of women	Women as a percentage of total union membership in 1978
APEX	45.0	116	56
ASTMS	67.8	721	18
AUEW (TASS)	24.2	691	14
COHSE	120.5	310	75
NALGO	186.7	141	45
NUPE	321.4	236	66
USDAW	114.9	74	61

Note:
APEX: Association of Professional Executive Clerical and Computer Staff
ASTMS: Association of Scientific, Technical and Managerial Staff
AUEW (TASS): Amalgamated Union of Engineering Workers (Technical Administrative and Supervisory Section)
COHSE: Confederation of Health Service Employees
NALGO: National Association of Local Government Officers
NUPE: National Union of Public Employees
USDAW Union of Shop, Distributive and Allied Workers
   Source: J. Hunt (1982), table 9.2.

Obviously, union membership among women closely reflects their position in a segmented labour market. In 1980, for example, over 70 per cent of total female membership was concentrated in just 10 unions and only 14 of the 117 unions affiliated to the TUC had a majority of women members (J. Hunt, 1982). These were unions representing workers in, for example, the public sector, textiles and clothing, retail and distribution, local government and school teaching. Thus, as J. Hunt points out,

> it was not inevitable that a numerical increase would be matched by an increased attention to policy and activity of women throughout the trade union movement, other than in a few unions. Indeed, a number of unions which had been traditionally high in female membership did not begin to develop their policies on women until the mid 1970s. (1982, pp. 158–9)

Male dominance within the union movement is reinforced by the chronic underrepresentation of women in executive or full-time official positions. This feature, 'common to all unions at all levels'

(Mackie and Patullo, 1977, p. 167), is often legitimated by men in terms of the conflict that women face between union demands and domestic responsibilities. Consequently, even in those unions where women predominate, the full-time officials, as Table 3.3 demonstrates, tend to be men.

Table 3.3   *Position of Women in Trade Unions, 1976*

Union	Women as a percentage of total union membership	No. of full-time officials	
		Male	Female
APEX	55	5	1
COHSE	70	35	5
NUPE	65	120	2
USDAW	59	129	4
NALGO	43	174	17

Source: J. Hunt (1982), table 9.3.

Trade unions in Britain, then, are overwhelmingly male institutions; men constitute more than 70 per cent of their total membership and virtually monopolize the senior official positions. This, in turn, is generally reflected in traditions, ideologies and interests of trade unionism. As Mackie and Patullo have remarked, 'The view of the man as rightful breadwinner and so the true unionist has tended to exclude women from enjoying full acceptance in unions. The mystique of a kind of male brotherhood is a strong feature of union history (1977, p. 173). Such traditions, of course, severely curtail the benefits of union membership for women. Male officials seem neither to fully understand nor sympathize with the particular problems which working women confront. To some extent, this is because of occupational segregation according to gender; very few men directly experience the nature of 'women's jobs' and they do not fully appreciate the problems associated with women's role in society (Cockburn, 1983).

It seems unlikely, therefore, that the trade union movement in Britain, with its present ideologies and objectives offers an appropriate means whereby women can improve their position in the labour market. Although women who do belong to trade unions tend to have better pay and working conditions than others, 'women's issues' remain marginal within the labour movement and subordinate to the overriding needs of male members. Further, trade unions have been unable to recruit women in those occupational sectors where they predominate as employees and where there are no traditions of collective organizations. A high proportion of them are employed in smaller enterprises and concentrated in lower-paid, part-time occupations which remain outside the influence of the labour movement. But if trade unionism has not adequately pursued the interests of women, has the women's movement, again with an emphasis upon collective organization, been able to achieve greater goals?

As J. Hunt has pointed out, the women's movement has few direct links with trade unionism. This is,

> partly because of the social composition of the movement, the separatist ideas of some sections of the movement, and because many of its activities consume time which is not available to working class women. Also trade unions traditionally do not have structural links with 'campaigning organisations' and at a local level there is suspicion of the new and rather challenging movement. (1982, p. 161)

The women's movement, of course, incorporates a diversity of ideologies ranging from liberal and reformist to revolutionary objectives (Sebastyen, 1979). In many countries, the right to vote was the first achievement of such collective action but this has been subsequently reinforced by moves towards greater legal equality in such areas as education, employment and property rights (Novarra, 1980). The legal nature of these reforms is to be emphasized since substantively, gender-based inequalities persist in each of these spheres (Reid and Wormald, eds, 1982). As a result, many groups within the women's movement emphasize the ineffectiveness of legal reform and stress the need for a fundamental restructuring of society if gender-based inequalities and the subordination of women is to be abolished. Hence, the overriding importance which the women's movement attaches to collective action. Indeed, sisterhood is seen as a fundamental principle of social organization. As Carden has argued:

> The concept of sisterhood is of great importance in the movement. If women are to cease living their lives through men, male friends and husbands should not play an exclusive role in a woman's life . . .

Those who believe in sexual equality must also believe that it is worthwhile 'really relating to' other women. (1974, pp. 14–15, quoted in
Oakley, 1982, p. 279)

Similarly, Mitchell accounts for the rationale of 'sisterhood' in the
following terms:

. . . it is women as a group that are oppressed . . . all Women's
Liberation politics act on the basis of developing collective work . . .
This . . . countermands both the hierarchic nature of the oppressive
society and the isolation and/or subservience that women are forced
into within the home and in their personal relationships . . .
Working together with other women in a united struggle overcomes
this isolation and competitiveness . . . The basic unit of organisation
. . . is the small group [which] is the means of bringing women into
close personal solidarity and friendship with each other . . . women's
problems are not private and personal, so, neither is their solution.
(1971, pp. 58–9)

The contemporary women's movement, then, is collectively based
and committed to 'consciousness-raising'. This encourages women
to share experiences and to 'feel that other women are truly sisters'
(Oakley, 1982, p. 280). Thus, priority is given to helping women
understand the social causes of their personal problems. It is, then,
assumed that collective action is essential if society is to be changed
and male-dominated institutions, structures and relationships are
to be destroyed. It is only then, so it is argued, that women will be
able to redefine their identity and achieve a greater degree of authen-
tic self-actualization. Through collective action, therefore, the
women's movement offers personal liberation. Hence, Delamont
has suggested that, 'the distinguishing characteristic of all feminists
is a desire that women be recognized "as individuals in their own
right". In other words, feminism is a desire for female self-
determination' (1980, p. 4).

However, it is difficult to assess the extent to which the women's
movement has been able to achieve many of its stated goals. There
are several reasons for this. First, unlike trade unions, the women's
movement does not have a clearly defined organizational structure.
As Morgan has remarked:

This is not a movement one 'joins'. There are no rigid structures or membership cards. The Women's Liberation Movement exists only where three or four friends or neighbours decide to meet regularly over coffee and talk about their personal lives. It also exists in the cells of women's jails, on the welfare lines, in the supermarket, the factory, the convent, the farm, the maternity ward, the street corner, the old ladies' home, the kitchen, the steno pool, the bed. It exists in your mind. (1970, p. xxvi, quoted in Oakley, 1982, pp. 308–9)

Secondly, because of its many ideologies, there are difficulties in determining the precise objectives of the women's movement. Although feminists are agreed upon the need for structural change in order to overcome their subordination, they differ as to the nature and the extent of such change; hence, the widespread debates within the movement (Evans, ed., 1982). Finally, many of the achievements which are often associated with the women's movement are not easily measurable. How is it possible to assess, for instance, the heightening of feminist consciousness or the achievement of self-determination? The attainment of such objectives cannot be evaluated on the kinds of indices commonly used in the study of trade union effectiveness.

Nevertheless, the women's movement has been influential in bringing about a range of social, economic and legal reforms which, at least to some extent, have improved the position of women and heightened public awareness of a number of gender-related inequalities. According to several feminist writers, one of the most notable achievements of the women's movement has been to highlight the manner in which the domestic division of labour is 'a primary (if not the prime) cause of women's subordination' (Evans, ed., 1982, p. 16). Thus, it is argued that without changes within this sphere, other reforms geared to improving the position of women are likely to flounder. Indeed, in her recent assessment of the women's movement Oakley concludes that it has altered commonly held assumptions of 'the political'. As she states:

Whatever else feminist politics have done in the last decade, they have broadened the concept of the political. In saying our politics begin with our feelings – rather than with our exercise of the franchise – feminists are drawing attention to the fact that the field of what is usually considered politics is a created one. Politics, in any and every sense, is about power, and it is as much about the power that men, wittingly or unwittingly, exercise over women as it is about the power that presidents and prime ministers wield over nations. (1982, p. 310)

In fact, it would not be an exaggeration to state that the major achievements of the women's movement have been outside the labour market; within it, rather like trade unions, it has achieved little in improving the occupational position of women.[1] To what extent, then, do individual as distinct from collective strategies offer greater possibilities?

As stated earlier, there are two major ways whereby women individually can tackle their subordination; namely, through the pursuit of careers and through business start-up. Given the concentration of women in lower-paid, secondary-sector occupations, the opportunities available for personal success through upward mobility within careers are likely to be severely restricted. Nevertheless, a small number of women do enter managerial and professional careers and occupy senior executive positions within large-scale corporations. Unfortunately, there are few studies of these successful women and the processes associated with their upward mobility are largely unexplored. Indeed, until recently, most investigators ignored the independent mobility experiences of women; their position within the class structure was assumed to be dependent upon that of either their fathers or their husbands (Parkin, 1971; Giddens, 1973; Goldthorpe, Llewellyn and Payne, 1980). Heath, however, is exceptional in comparing the separate occupational achievements of men and women and suggests,

that women have considerably poorer mobility chances than men – if we take their own occupational achievements rather than their husbands' as the yardstick. They are more likely to be downwardly mobile and less likely to be upwardly mobile than men from the same class origins. And this, of course, is due to their enormous concentration in 'women's work' – their employment as secretaries, shop assistants, clerks, telephone operators, waitresses, cooks and hairdressers. (1981, p. 117)

Of course, some men argue that many women choose part-time, less-demanding work because they prefer, as a life ambition, to be married and to bring up children. But such a view ignores the considerable social pressures which 'force' women to conform to stereotyped, conventional female roles. In fact, women need to possess a considerable degree of assertiveness if they are to reject firmly established ideologies which encourage them to accept their traditional roles as mothers and wives (Larwood and Wood, 1977). Further, many women are likely to give priority to domestic responsibilities if only because of the very limited opportunities available to them within the labour market. Thus, they deliberately choose part-time employment and regard this as secondary to their familial obligations (Sanders and Reid, 1982). This, in turn, sustains a pattern of severely restricted occupational opportunities for women.

Despite these strong social pressures, some women do give priority to the pursuit of occupational careers and explicitly choose to avoid marriage and its associated domestic responsibilities. What, then, are their mobility chances compared with those of single men? Heath claims that although women are still under-represented at very senior managerial and professional levels 'the present data suggest . . . . that single women have been able to make use of such opportunities as are available to them *to obtain jobs of generally higher social standing than their male equivalents*' (1981, p. 12, italics added). However, this does not deny the generally limited career opportunities which are available to women by comparison with men. Rather, it suggests that the values and aspirations of single women may differ markedly from both their married counterparts and from single men. As Heath goes on to argue:

> For most men the choice of work or marriage does not present itself as a dilemma; the two are complementary not antagonistic. But for most women it is a dilemma. The typical role-expectations confronting a wife and mother reduce her ability to pursue a career effectively. She cannot usually maximise her contributions in one role without sacrificing those in the other. This suggests that the woman who actually does opt for a career by staying single may have a greater commitment to work than the single man who has not had to make the same sacrifices . . . The single woman, therefore, may well differ markedly from the married woman in their greater occupational ambitions; but there is no reason to expect that the single men differ likewise from their married counterparts. (1981, p. 123)

Unfortunately, there is little information about the experiences of women in careers. But a recent study of women managers in British industry by Cooper and Davidson does provide some insights. In particular, they found that women managers are more prone than men to stress, a characteristic which is derived from their lack of role models, feelings of personal isolation, experiences of gender-based discrimination and, for married women, tensions associated with combining work and domestic roles. The repercussions of these factors, when combined with other management-related sources of tension, can be severe and the authors found a high incidence of sleeplessness, smoking, alcohol consumption and diminished levels of job performance among the women whom they studied. They conclude that by comparison to men, 'career women face additional stressors which subject them to even higher levels of work-related stress' (1982, p. 201).

Clearly, the opportunities available for women to pursue managerial and professional careers remain highly limited. For most, therefore, paid employment does not offer them a means for overcoming subordination; the world of work merely confirms the deprivations which they encounter in their family and domestic roles. For the small, but increasing number who do pursue careers, the personal costs would appear to be high. Comparative studies of both career men and women are needed in order to determine the similarities and differences in their occupational experiences (Davidson and Cooper, 1983b).

If the pursuit of careers within organizations poses problems for women, the entrepreneurial strategy offers an alternative route for those who wish to escape their conditions of economic and social subordination. Within capitalist economies, members of ethnic and religious minorities have often started their own businesses as a means of accumulating capital and achieving personal upward mobility (Stanworth and Curran, 1973). Business proprietorship, in other words, offers opportunities for those who, because of prejudice and other reasons, are unable to gain entry into different salaried, middle-class occupations or who are altogether excluded from employment. However, it is important to bear in mind that the opportunities available for self-employment and small-scale proprietorship vary considerably between different sectors of the economy (Scase and Goffee, 1982, Ch. 2). Where production is labour intensive as, for example, in the handicraft and clothing industries, conditions are particularly favourable for small business start-up. Similarly, within the personal services sector, retailing and the 'informal economy' the conditions are conducive to the formation of small-scale enterprises. Even so, business proprietorship does not offer an open avenue for individual upward mobility in the sense of amassing large amounts of capital. On the contrary, the majority of those who embark upon entrepreneurial ventures remain self-employed with no employees, experiencing high risks, long working hours and receiving relatively low rewards (Scase and Goffee, 1981). But for those whose businesses expand beyond self-employment how is personal success to be measured? By contrast to organizational careers where personal achievement can be determined according to upward movement between clearly defined occupational categories, entrepreneurial success cannot be so readily measured by such identifiable indices. Conventional measures, such as the number of employees, capital assets utilized and the level of turnover, provide only a limited understanding of the underlying dynamics of business proprietorship. Consequently, for the purposes of studying entrepreneurial careers, it is necessary to categorize different types of business proprietor. It is possible to identify four such types (Goffee and Scase, 1983b). First, there are *self-employed* who work for themselves and formally employ no labour. However, they are often dependent upon the unpaid services of others, particularly other family members (Scase and Goffee, 1980b). Secondly, there are *small-employers* who not only work alongside their employees but also undertake the administrative and managerial tasks associated with running their businesses (Scase and Goffee, 1982). Thirdly, there are the *owner-controllers* who do not work alongside their employees but, instead, are solely and singularly responsible for the administration and management of their enterprises (Scase and Goffee, 1982, Ch. 6). Finally, there are *owner-directors* who own and control companies with management hierarchies and within which executive decision-making is delegated to senior managerial staff (Goffee and Scase, 1984). Although such a categorization is based upon the roles of business owners, nevertheless it provides a useful index of the general nature of their enterprises since it reflects, for example, size of labour force and level of trading. Entrepreneurial success, then, can be measured in terms of mobility between these categories. There are, however, a number of obstacles that prevent or restrict movement between them (Scase and Goffee, 1983). Although some may be associated with financial and market factors, those related to the employment of staff can also be important. The self-employed and small-employers, for example, often lack the necessary skills for the supervision of employees that small-business growth normally entails. This usually applies to those who engage in entrepreneurial ventures because they are unable to obtain secure employment or pursue careers within large-scale organizations. Thus, female proprietors are likely to be either self-employed or small-employers. The self-employed trade with their craft, professional, or technical skills and, as a result, frequently lack the necessary managerial competence required for the supervision of staff. Small-employers encounter similar problems which limit their potential for business growth. They tend to adopt a style of close, face-to-face supervision which inherently restricts their potential for business growth. Consequently, few small businesses expand to any great size. It is not surprising, therefore, to find that the greatest concentration of women proprietors is among the self-employed and small-employers. Recent evidence for the United States, for example, suggests that over 70 per cent of all businesses owned by women had no employees; more than 60 per cent were financed from the owners' personal savings, and almost 50 per cent were operated from the proprietor's homes (US Department of Commerce, 1980, p. 5).

What, then, are the characteristics of those women who start their own businesses? There is very little data on these issues in Britain but surveys conducted in the United States during the 1970s provide some information. These suggest that most women proprietors 'have been in the workforce for several years prior to starting their own businesses, had created – not inherited – their businesses, and had started their businesses alone – without a partner or spouse' (Interagency Task Force on Women Business Owners, 1978, p. 5). Somewhat more strikingly, only 27 per cent of women business owners in the United States are currently married, despite the fact that over 60 per cent are more than 44 years old (US Department of Commerce, 1980, pp. 5–8). Most of these women tend to come from business backgrounds, using their parents as 'role models'. The United States evidence suggests that the reasons why women start their own businesses are similar to those of men, 'to make money, to be their own boss, and to use a skill' (Interagency Task Force on Women Business Owners, 1978, p. 34). Further, the 'successful' female entrepreneur, 'comes from a close, supportive family, exhibits a strong entrepreneurial drive, is persistent in her approach to work-related tasks and has an uncanny ability to redirect negative situations and attitudes to her advantage' (Interagency Task Force on Women Business Owners, 1978, p. 5). But how many women proprietors are really success-ful in running their own ventures? It would seem that most encounter gender-related difficulties which can severely threaten the viability of their businesses. As the Interagency Task Force on Women Business Owners has stated,

> discrimination limits the options and success of the potential woman entrepreneur. It narrows the number of fields she may choose to enter, deprives her of management skills and knowledge, and reduces her ability to accumulate sufficient collateral and the management track record she needs for financing. Most important, it diminishes the perception of her management credibility to start and conduct her own business . . . After months of research and evaluation, the Task Force has concluded that if starting a new business is considered difficult, it is considerably more difficult for a woman. A systemic history of overt discrimination starts her on a course in life that steers her from a traditional 'man's province', prevents her from training for careers that lead to entrepreneurship, diminishes her ambitions and aspirations for this career, and then places obstacles in her path as she tries to pursue it. (1978, pp. 5, 7)

Clearly, then, the 'American dream' of independent business pro-prietorship is one which only a few women have so far been able to realize. Yet in the United States there are signs of an increase in the incidence of female proprietorship. Between 1977 and 1980, for example, the number of women-owned enterprises in the United States increased by 33 per cent and the most rapid growth areas were in traditionally male-dominated sectors of the economy (manufacturing, mining, finance and real estate) where the inci-dence of female entrepreneurship has always been extremely low (US Small Business Administration, 1983, p. 315). Although the absolute numbers are small, this is a remarkable increase; certainly by comparison with trends in Britain and other European countries.

Evidence from studies in the United States suggests that women who are successful in establishing their own businesses obtain benefits which extend beyond the purely economic. In fact, they seem to measure personal success according to different criteria to men. In a study conducted in 1977 one woman remarked, 'My success is different from that of businessmen. My experience is that they [men] look at the dollar volume only.' By contrast, the report indicates that women experience a greater 'sense of self-worth, often not present in earlier stages of their development. This was manifested in an increased self-confidence, a factor that many believed was a contributory element to their success. A number . . . observed that women are hindered by cultural stereotypes and expectations that result in reduced levels of confidence' (Interagency Task Force on Women Business Owners, 1978, p. 216). Such observations, then, suggest that proprietorship can offer women possibilities for self-determination and enable them to overcome their subordination. Indeed, in the United States, government agencies which have been established to encourage small businesses among ethnic minority groups apply similar criteria in their dealings with intending women proprietors. [2] There is some evidence that the women's movement supports this policy.

In Britain, by contrast, feminists have generally rejected business proprietorship as a means whereby women can combat their subordination in the labour market (Novarra, 1980). Primarily, it seems, this is because proprietorship is seen to foster capitalist values and institutions which, in turn, sustain the domination of men over women. Further, many feminists assume that with the possible exception of women's co-operatives, proprietorship undermines the collective means of sisterhood and that any degree of self-determination enjoyed by a few female proprietors does little to improve the material conditions of the oppressed from whose ranks they have emerged. Thus, the personal gains of these women merely serve to sustain a structure which confines most women to their subordinate positions.

It can be argued, however, that such a view rests upon a

stereotyped image of both conventional and co-operative proprietorship which neglects their radical potential. First, setting up a small business does not necessarily constitute a personal reaffirmation of the principles of capital accumulation; on the contrary, it can represent an explicit rejection of the exploitative nature of the capitalist work process and labour market (Scase and Goffee, 1981). In this sense, then, business proprietorship may be seen as a radical – albeit short-term and individualistic – response to subordination. Secondly, even though some women business owners are committed to the virtues of private ownership and profit, their position may query the traditionally defined, gender-based division of labour (Goffee and Scase, 1983a, 1983c). Thus, women who both own and manage business enterprises – especially those in male-dominated sectors of the economy – serve to undermine conventional and stereotyped notions of 'a woman's place'.[3] Female entrepreneurs such as these, therefore, have a symbolic importance which explicitly questions popular conceptions of the position of women in society. Finally, proprietorship can enable women to enjoy some material independence and, in many circumstances, the opportunity to control the products of their own labour. In some developing countries, for instance, women market traders have been able to obtain a degree of material independence from men which can provide a basis for female solidarity (Caplan, 1978). In such cases, individualism fosters collective action rather than preventing it. In her analysis of women beer producers in Kenya, for example, Nelson notes that,

> Individual entrepreneurs utilise their personal networks to survive by illegal petty commodity production in an uncertain market. This daily economic co-operation supports a wider solidarity among these women. Feeling themselves isolated from and stigmatised by the larger society, because of their deviant behaviour and economic independence, they express a need to stand together as women against common enemies. These enemies are perceived and articulated as either agents of authority, for example, the police, or men in general. (1978, p. 77)

There are, then, various collective and individual strategies available to women who wish to overcome their experience of subordination both within the labour market and in the wider society. In the remaining chapters of this book we devote more detailed attention to one of these, that of proprietorship. What, then, are the motives for, and the consequences of, business ownership for women and to what extent does it enable them to achieve a greater degree of self-determination?

Notes: Chapter 3

1 In making this statement we recognize that the spheres of unpaid domestic labour and paid employment cannot be separated; indeed, that relationships of dominance and subordination within the domestic sphere serve to sustain and reinforce those within the labour market (and vice versa) (Stanworth, 1984). However, at the time of writing, the direct impact of the women's movement upon the division of labour within paid work has been negligible.
2 We refer to the Women's Business Enterprise Division of the Small Business Administration (Interagency Committee on Women's Business Enterprise, 1980).
3 A similar assertion can be made concerning women who succeed in managerial and professional careers.

4

The Work and Life-Styles of Female Proprietors: some Preliminary Findings

In order to investigate the experiences, attitudes and life-styles of women business owners we conducted loosely structured, taped interviews with fifty-four female proprietors, between 1981 and 1983.[1] We contacted these women in non-random fashion, using personal recommendations, business directories and media publicity. The intention was to include women from the various 'service', 'professional' and 'craft' sectors (discussed in Chapter 2) where most female proprietors are concentrated. Consequently, interviews were conducted with women who were running businesses in, for example, various retail sectors, catering, cleaning, accommodation (guest houses), secretarial and clerical services, professional services (advertising, market research, public relations), and craftwork (dressmaking, pottery, engraving). Most of these businesses were relatively small-scale with less than twenty employees and most had been established within the previous twenty years. However, a small number of women running relatively large businesses were also included so that the final selection ranged from home-based, self-employed proprietors to owner-managers of international enterprises. However, all the women had founded or co-founded their businesses and, at the time of interview, were directly involved in the day-to-day management of them. Almost three-quarters of the women were in their thirties or forties but only twenty-eight were married or co-habiting when contacted. In all, thirty of the women had children. More detailed biographies and business data are provided in each of the following four chapters.

In conducting these interviews we did not attempt to achieve a representative sample; rather, the intention was to collect a detailed set of personal accounts which could help to illustrate the motives for, and consequences of, female proprietorship in a variety of contexts.[2] We begin the analysis here and pursue it on the basis of an emergent typology which is described at the end of this chapter and elaborated in Part Two of the book. Throughout there is considerable emphasis upon the actual statements (drawn from the tape transcripts) of the women we interviewed. This is a technique we have applied and defended elsewhere in analyses of male entrepreneurs (Scase and Goffee, 1982, 'Methodological appendix'). For the purpose of illustration in the context of exploratory research it acts as a useful reporting device. But, more importantly, the direct reproduction of first-hand accounts represents perhaps the most effective way to convey the richness, subtlety and ambiguity of individual experiences.

We began all the interviews with a discussion of the motives for business start-up and these indicated that women established their own enterprises for a variety of reasons. In some cases, there is little real choice; proprietorship is a 'last resort' because of the impossibility of obtaining adequately paid employment in the labour market. Many single women with children are often only able to take part-time paid employment because they need flexible hours for their family commitments (Mackie and Patullo, 1977; Hurstfield, 1978). However, such occupations are usually poorly paid and insufficient to meet the financial commitments of those with no access to a second 'male' income. Thus, starting a business is often seen to be a means whereby an income can be obtained in a manner compatible with other obligations. Two of the women explained the reasons for starting their own businesses in these terms:

I had turned 40 and at that time, as a woman secretary, you were dead at 35. You didn't get interviews . . . I would have done anything to get a job but I was being offered jobs at under £2,000 . . . and I had two kids I was rearing on my own . . . Going into business I was desperately trying to earn a living to keep my kids. I didn't see it as a great golden opportunity to make money at all. I wasn't a woman entrepreneur, I was a mother struggling to keep two children. My reality was to pay my rent and keep my kids. That was my only reality at that stage.

I had a broken marriage and teenaged children. I'd come back from fifteen years abroad . . . and I'd got no qualifications . . . I needed to work but I believed that a mother should be at home for children where possible . . . I was a woman who needed to support myself financially but it was very difficult for me to work part-time. It just happened that I had the opportunity of developing what I found [into a business].

Other women claimed they had started their own businesses because of various unsatisfactory experiences associated with being employees. More specifically, proprietorship offers an opportunity to escape from employer and managerial-imposed control systems of the workplace. Here, there are parallels with the motives of men who start their own businesses because they want to obtain a greater degree of personal working autonomy (Scase and Goffee, 1980a, 1981, 1982). Several women stressed the importance of this as the motive for small business start-up.

I was bored in my job . . . there was a deep-seated wish to go out . . . and be my own boss. I always had that in mind . . . I didn't want to take instructions from somebody else; I wanted to organize the whole thing myself.

I didn't want to work for anybody else. I like the freedom of this . . . When you're working for other people you could really work hard . . . and get no credit for it. Then, the minute you ease up . . . everyone's down on you like a ton of bricks: 'What are you doing?' 'Why aren't you working?'

I was totally at the mercy of other people's whims and fancies . . . I suddenly thought I would set up on my own. I thought I couldn't possibly make a worse hash of my life than everybody else was making for me . . . I'd had it working with other people. I was either going to be a wage slave for the rest of my life or be entirely my own boss . . . [Now] I love not having anyone telling me what to do.

I didn't want to work for somebody else. I wanted the satisfaction of doing something for myself . . . the satisfaction of thinking, 'I set that up and if I hadn't thought about it, it wouldn't be there'.

For many, the dislike of paid employment is associated with the reality or perception of discrimination in the labour market which restricts most women to lower-paid, less-skilled jobs with limited career prospects (A. Hunt, 1975). Thus, the frustrations of paid work are often seen to be associated with male-dominated control structures which operate against the interests of women (Fogarty, Allen and Walters, 1981; Davidson and Cooper, 1983b). Those who have been in direct competition with men for promotion are likely to refer to this factor as a major reason for starting their own businesses. One woman made the following comments in explaining her motives:

> A woman has got to be better than a man. If a man and a woman are up for the same job – both of equal ability – the man is always going to get it. I knew I had gone as far as I was ever going to go . . . As a woman there was never any way I was going to get any higher.

In a similar manner, an important factor for many women is the wish to avoid subordination within the domestic sphere. Several of the married women claimed that having their own businesses gave them economic and social independence and a means of self-expression which they were denied as housewives. As three of them told us:

> My husband always put me down terribly and made me feel stupid. I think I really wanted to prove myself – not so much to him as to *myself* because he took all my self-confidence away . . . If I wanted anything I always had to ask my husband . . . I had no money of my own and I think that's very degrading for a woman. So it's really a matter of being independent. I love to be independent.

> Although I suppose I was quite happy being just a wife and a mother for the first twelve years of my marriage, I was looking ahead to the future. Would I still be happy staying at home, doing the gardening and the cleaning for the next thirty years? I wanted something else to do . . . something constructive. I didn't want to turn round when I was 70 and have nothing to show at the end of it.

> I'd got two children and a home to run and a husband who had his own business. My children were getting a bit older. I had to put my energies somewhere. I've got a lot of energy . . . and I'd spent ten years in this line of work. It's a waste not to use something you realize you know quite a lot about.

Many single women also recognize that proprietorship offers a preferable alternative to either the dependent status of housewife or low-paid employee. One recalled:

> I wanted to be independent. I didn't want to get married. I was only 22. I could either start my own business or find some rich person to marry or win a lot of money! I just wanted to be financially independent. You've got to be able to say 'I want to go this place, do that thing', without relying on anyone else for your income.

It would be wrong, however, to assume that the desire for self-expression always implies a rejection of traditional family and domestic roles. For some women, business proprietorship is seen as a way of combining work with domestic obligations and as a means of strengthening family relationships. This view was expressed by one woman in the following terms:

> I think it stimulates a marriage if a woman is working. She becomes more interesting and the man is more satisfied in the end. It takes away a lot of the bitterness . . . I must say where a husband and wife are doing their own thing it makes for a much more satisfactory marriage

These accounts, then, illustrate the many different problems which women attempt to overcome through business start-up. Although many are associated with gender-related disadvantages, few women explicitly describe the decision to start their own enterprises in these terms. Nevertheless, there are a small number who consciously interpret their actions as attempts to combat male dominance in a more general sense. One proprietor, for example, expressed her feelings as follows:

> I'm in a man's business because I want to prove I'm as good as they are. In fact, I want to prove I'm better . . . I have a fantasy of driving a Rolls Royce and picking up men and saying 'Ha, ha, I've got a Rolls Royce, don't you wish you had one!' Just to put men in their little places. I suppose it's really because men dominate women. I've been dominated by men, so I just enjoy achieving the things men want to achieve – and doing it better than them . . . The whole reason I'm in business stems back really to my feelings about men and my role in

the world and my status and what I think of men. That's why I'm doing it.

Whereas this proprietor was conducting a personal campaign to 'beat men at their own game', others explicitly regard their businesses as part-and-parcel of the women's movement. As such, political rather than economic considerations are paramount. As one co-owner explained:

> It is very important to mention . . . that we set ourselves up explicitly as a *political* venture. We had no idea at all whether we would actually manage in business terms, this was very much a secondary consideration . . . It was a complete leap in the dark financially . . . [but] we do not see ourselves primarily as a business . . . we are a result of the women's movement that has been taking place over the last ten years. Without the agitation that has gone before, without the analysis, without the political activity, we could not exist.

It is clear, then, that women become business proprietors for a number of different reasons. Of course, all small businesses have to be economically viable. At the start-up stage, for instance, all proprietors – whether they are women or men – must be committed to generating profits.[3] But, as with men, there are also various other motives shaping business start-up among women. In some cases, the business is seen simply as a way of generating a greater income than could be obtained through employment; in others, it represents a vehicle for married women to express craft skills without neglecting domestic responsibilities. But for a significant number of them, as with men, proprietorship is linked to the quest for personal autonomy and self-expression. As such, it is regarded as a means whereby it is possible to escape the supervisory controls of formal employment and/or the inhibiting constraints of domestic relationships. In a broader sense, then, it offers women the possibility of rejecting male-imposed identities which are allocated to them within various social institutions. But how far are such objectives actually achieved through proprietorship?

Although business ownership offers women the potential of financial independence, the extent to which this is actually achieved largely depends upon the availability of credit and the amount of profit which the enterprise generates. Even though the women we interviewed are concentrated in fairly labour-intensive sectors of the economy, few possessed the necessary financial resources for complete economic independence at the start of trading. Personal savings were rarely sufficient to avoid the need for 'outside' financial assistance. Consequently, aspiring female entrepreneurs often approach the banks for loan facilities. Most women described the bank's reactions to their requests as generally unsympathetic and patronizing. They claimed that this response was based less upon a rational consideration of the financial viability of proposals than a more general 'biased' opinion of women's ability to own and control businesses. The following comments are illustrative:

> My bank manager was almost open-mouthed when I first went to see him. 'I don't believe this! A woman starting off in business . . .' Up until quite recently he just didn't take me seriously.

> With bank managers there's two things to be said. One, they're nicer to you because you're a woman. Two, they're worse because they think you're stupid.

> They see women as pretty and frivolous and not to be taken too seriously . . . Older bank managers tend to look at you as their younger daughter: 'What's a nice young thing like you wanting to do a thing like this for? Aren't you better staying at home?' One manager actually likened me to his daughter which was infuriating.

Such reactions by financial institutions can have real material consequences for women proprietors. Thus, in some instances, they are compelled to have male business partners for the purposes of negotiating credit and for acting as financial guarantors. But while such strategies can be successful for obtaining credit, this may be at the expense of personal financial independence. Thus, 'sleeping' male partners who perform no active day-to-day tasks in the running of women's businesses may, even so, claim a share of the profits and continue to act as the gatekeepers for further credit. As a result of this, some female proprietors do 'buy out' their male partners once their businesses are flourishing. However, as one of them explained, this can be expensive.

Someone came out of the blue and offered to finance me. So I had financial backing for two years. [He] was an elderly merchant banker who had a totally eighteenth-century attitude . . . It cost me a great deal of money to throw him out. But I was lucky – and he *did* finance me. It cost me a lot more to buy him out than he put into it. He gambled on it and I was lucky. But it didn't work because he wanted to run it on one level and I wanted to do it my way.

Such difficulties can lead both aspiring and established proprietors to seek financial help from less 'formal' sources, namely, families, friends and acquaintances. But, again, such credit comes almost entirely from men and it typically entitles them to participate in business decision-making and planning. Further, these informal arrangements often increase the risk of women losing their highly valued proprietorial independence to men who manipulate matters to their own advantage. One respondent described her own 'equal' partnership with a male friend as follows:

I think he takes advantage of me. I know he's doing it. I know when he's doing it. But I can't stop him. I don't like it – and I don't see any way out. In fact, the idea of my having this business of my own, initially, was so I could get away from him. I strove to become independent of him. But when it actually came to the crunch, things had got too big for me and I knew I couldn't manage it on my own . . . I felt safer with him around – with his knowledge and experience. Plus, the finance that he's bringing in. So I accept that this is the price I've got to pay for it . . . I can, a man couldn't. There's no way any man – unless he was a doormat – could work as a partner with him. He would never, ever be an equal partner.

These examples illustrate the vulnerability of women within a male-dominated economic system. Because women are often seen by men to lack business 'credibility' they can have difficulties in obtaining credit and, as a result, be forced to use men as financial partners. But the trading autonomy of women proprietors can be further restricted in other spheres. Although many women's businesses have only female employees, in enterprises where there are men, women have either to develop 'appropriate' managerial strategies to legitimate their authority or, alternatively, delegate supervisory responsibilities to male intermediaries. Often the latter is the easier in view of the persistence of prejudice among men about working for women (Kanter, 1981). But this can involve a loss of proprietorial control over business operations. As one woman explained:

> I do find it difficult . . . you don't speak the same language as boys . . . My partner is better with the boys . . . men and boys speak the same language – women don't. I know that one or two of them think a woman's place is in the home. They don't think I should be telling *them* what to do anyway . . . Maybe again it's my inferiority complex or lack of confidence but I think they probably have got more respect for him than for me because he's a man . . . he's always really been the big boss.

But even women who are directly responsible for supervision are, like female managers, sometimes forced to adopt strategies which constrain their proprietorial role (Kanter, 1977; Bartol, 1980; Cooper and Davidson, 1982). Several claimed that they often had to act as 'mother' in order to develop close, 'trusting' relationships, and yet, at the same time, maintain a degree of social distance from their employees. The following comments are illustrative of the 'maternal image' which was evoked by several proprietors.

> Employees want straight talking . . . It's like being a mother and dealing with children . . . You have to play games with them and you have to play games with people.

> You have to act as a mother . . . a confessor. Someone that they will come to and who will understand. But someone who will also be able to judge the people you like to 'carrot' and those you have to 'beat' . . . to get the best work out of them.

Similarly, in dealing with customers and suppliers, women business owners are often forced to exploit their female identity. They can be compelled to use, for example, 'feminine attraction' in order to negotiate sales and many claimed this was the most appropriate way of clinching business deals. Indeed, feelings about the use of such tactics vary from a positive instrumental acceptance to strong personal unease, as the following comments illustrate.

Clients are very surprised when they find I'm a woman . . . When they find out I'm in charge. I think it puts them off for a little while . . . I guess they think I should be at home rearing children . . . If you think it's going to help, you can be charming to a man . . . especially if it's going to make the difference between getting a sale and not getting one. The fact that you're a woman and nice – it's just another tool in the repertoire really.

Sometimes you've *got* to give someone 'the eye' or the 'come-on'. I can do all those things. So, as a woman, I have got certain assets on the sexual side . . . as a woman dealing with men.

I do have to put up with a certain amount of sexism from some of the men that I have to deal with . . . You know, those little jokes and little innuendoes which are a bit boring . . . it's quite a lot to do with the kind of vocabulary and play that sales people engage in . . . [but] I can't stand here with my hand on my heart and say I don't respond . . . I make quite a lot of effort in terms of the way I dress and present myself in certain sorts of situations.

If women experience tensions in their business dealings, these can be reinforced, certainly for those who are married, by the conflicting demands of work and the family. Many husbands expect their wives to perform a range of household tasks despite the demands of their businesses. When asked about her husband's attitudes to the business, one woman replied:

His attitude at the beginning was 'Well, as long as you're here and I have my dinner and the house runs, I don't mind'. That, to me, was the most frightening aspect of the whole thing.

Indeed, the interviews suggested that husbands rarely contribute to the running of either homes or businesses. This contrasts strongly with the experience of male proprietors; as we have shown elsewhere, many male-owned enterprises could not survive without the unpaid contribution of wives who, in addition, are forced to be single-handedly responsible for the family and the home (Scase and Goffee, 1980b and 1982, chs 4 and 5). But female proprietors do not seem to receive comparable help from their husbands except, possibly, as financial partners. Consequently, some women — instead of enjoying a greater degree of personal autonomy through business ownership — can often feel even more severely constrained by irreconcilable demands. As two respondents confessed:

> I think we're mad. We've dug this enormous hole for ourselves. I'm a wife, lover, mother and businesswoman. It's just impossible! I can't be all things! Something has to go . . . so much of your emotion is taken in running your business you've just got nothing over.

> The business has got to the stage where my husband has slightly clamped down. He often says he'd prefer it if I didn't work in the evenings. But it's trying to balance the children and the job and my household duties . . . every mum who works feels semi-guilty about the fact that they ought to be spending every living, waking hour with their children. I feel I've done the very best I can . . . although I sometimes wonder.

Clearly many of the difficulties faced by female proprietors stem from the fact that they are seen to lack the credibility that men have as business owners. (For similar evidence on the 'credibility gap' experienced by women managers see Kanter, 1977; Larwood and Wood, 1977; Hennig and Jardim, 1979; Cooper and Davidson, 1982.) Bank managers, customers, employees and husbands do not always grant businesswomen the same esteem and competence they accord to men. Further, as entrepreneurs, they are sometimes regarded as 'unusual' since they do not adhere to traditional, male-defined notions of the female role. Those proprietors whose business dealings brought them mainly into contact with men were more acutely aware of these problems than others. As three of them explained:

> People are amused . . . They're prepared almost to say 'Well, I suppose there's always room for freaks, isn't there?' That makes them feel a bit better.

> Men are terrified of you. Absolutely terrified when they discover you own a business. I used to think, 'Why don't any of these guys ask you out?' . . . It's because they don't know how to handle me. I'm a sort of strange monster.

It's very difficult for men to accept me . . . I'm a threat because I run my own business. I don't need them for anything.

If some women are conscious of their 'odd' identity, others – more firmly committed to the feminist movement and to the need to restructure gender relationships – are acutely aware of the contradictions of trading in an economy which sustains the subordination of women. As two admitted:

Having to survive as a capitalist enterprise and being a women's movement thing – the problems are acute. I never had such problems in my job before . . . The system in which we survive is a capitalist system and we can transform pockets of it – but I don't really see how we can pose real alternatives given that we are people who live by buying and selling and selling and buying. That's what our business is . . . sometimes you can't be that nice – you have to know what your priorities are and that is a very painful thing; to know that the survival of what you've put so much work into depends on *not* being nice . . . Because we're not a little collective making stickers or badges or doing anything terribly nice and 'wholemealy'. We are a business with a big turnover, a big debt and lots of things to be decided very fast.

We do feel ourselves to be answerable to the women's movement, and that is our conscience. We are feminists . . . [but] we can't get away from the fact that we do operate as a business. And, of course, we have had criticism about that from the women's movement. But we have undertaken to sell goods . . . You actually have to deal in barter of some kind if you're going to transfer goods. Right from the beginning we said . . . that we *do* wish to pay ourselves wages and that the enterprise had failed if it didn't pay us.

To sum up the experiences of these women, it would seem that the reality of business proprietorship does not always conform to expectations. Although they often seek personal autonomy they can become dependent upon others, and particularly men, for finance and various technical and professional services. In striving for self-determination, they often become even more burdened with domestic and business responsibilities. As Bechhofer and his colleagues (1974b) have suggested, small-scale business ownership promises 'autonomy' but, in actual fact, it offers 'serfdom'. Such an observation appears particularly appropriate for some women proprietors. But despite the difficulties which they encounter, few seem to regret the decision to start their own businesses.[4] Indeed, their accounts suggest that proprietorship offers several unanticipated rewards. The prejudices they encounter from men, for example, may exaggerate their trading difficulties but, at the same time, this can contribute to the development of a greater awareness of the general problems associated with women's subordination. Herein lies a possible contradiction in the experience of female entrepreneurship in a male-dominated economy. One of the women expressed this when she claimed:

> I wouldn't say that I was a great women's libber; it wasn't a big thing in my life. But, definitely, doing this job has made me more like that. I've started realizing how deeply that kind of prejudice goes. I was vaguely aware of it before. I'm very aware of it now . . . we get men to like us – get them to do business with us . . . we get around them and we get them to knock down their prices. Why not? Someone once said to me, 'That's not fair!' But we've had it hard enough for so long. We want to get something out of it. Get our own back. At the moment men have all the advantages, so any advantage that we can get we'll take. I don't regard it as a war, but there have been little battles and we point them out . . . There are definitely problems for women in business which men don't have . . . [A woman partner] is someone on my side who'll sympathize with me. And we can have a little moan together about men who don't take us seriously. It is 'them' and 'us'.

For her, the experience of running a business also demonstrates the need for women to take more positive action in changing their position.

> Personally, I think that women can be their own worst enemies. They can sit around complaining about men without actually *doing* something about it to change it. You can't make other people change by telling them to think of you differently. You've got to *show* them you're different.

Further, women may also acquire new talents as a result of entrepreneurship. In the following example, the importance of obtaining financial expertise as a means of overcoming subordination was only fully appreciated through the experience of proprietorship.

> I've always enjoyed understanding the financial side of the whole business . . . women are treated as second-class citizens and the most efficient way of keeping us in that situation is to deny us access to money and to knowledge of how it works and to keep it, literally, in men's hands . . . It's given me enormous satisfaction to see the bank manager crawl . . . I have a greater insight now because I've actually come into contact with making money work for *us* in a way that *we* want it to.

However, the greatest gain derived from business ownership appears to be an increase in personal self-confidence and, despite the obstacles, a greater feeling of personal autonomy. For many women these gains may be entirely compatible with their other, more conventional roles as housewives and mothers. As one of them stated:

> Working for yourself you can keep your life under control much better. You're not beholden to other people . . . I hope in future more women do it – there'd be a lot less waiting in doctors' waiting rooms for valium and everything else. If you've got an interest it's lovely and if you can earn some money as well that's great . . . you get independence and freedom and get a bit more money into the house . . . For me, working for myself gives me control over my life and, especially, it fits in with the kids. My husband certainly approves of it.

But for other women, proprietorship offers them possibilities for rejecting their social and psychological subordination. As two of them commented:

> Women don't think of themselves . . . They're brought up to be provided for by a man . . . Nobody ever says 'You can do this' to a woman . . . It's just, 'Get on with all this dogsbodying' . . . Why won't women try to run businesses? What is it they're missing? We're not encouraged to think of *ourselves*. To think we're confident enough to do it. That's all it is really, *confidence*.

> Women will always put up an excuse that they can't do it because they haven't got the time, and they've got children, they've got aged parents, they've got something or the other. If you *want* to do things you can do them!

In other words, despite the obstacles, compromises and difficulties, proprietorship demonstrates in very real ways to many women the potential of strength through self-determination. This is, perhaps its most significant consequence. As several of the women pointed out:

> I learnt to think, 'What do *I* want? *Me*. Where am I going with my life?' I tried not to let men interfere with it . . . Too many women are swamped. All they are is 'mum' and 'wife' but never themselves.

> The business was a great liberator for me in a way because I thought, 'I've done all this on my own'. And it's quite a brave thing to do. It takes a lot of confidence and a lot of nerve. You are living just by your own efforts . . . I began to realize my own worth. That's one thing that does hold women back an awful lot.

> The business has taught me to be totally strong about myself. Not to expect my husband to be part or half of my life . . . I make sure I'm strong in myself and true to myself – and try not to unload any of myself onto him – if we came unstuck I wouldn't be devastated.

From these findings, then, it is evident that business start-up does not offer women an easy route to personal autonomy. They often find it difficult to obtain full credibility as proprietors and they become dependent upon creditors, customers and husbands in a way which can seriously erode their independence. Nevertheless, the interviews indicate that proprietorship can heighten their understanding of women's subordination and lead them to query the prevailing structure of gender roles. It is, however, important to stress that, as the interviews suggest, there is no single experience of proprietorship. Motivations for start-up and the consequences of business ownership vary considerably. What, then, are the factors accounting for these?

Obviously, there are a range of influences shaping the start-up process and the subsequent business outcomes (Gorb, 1981). The age, education, family background and occupational experience of proprietors are important and, for women in particular, their marital status and domestic commitments would seem to be significant. Further, business opportunities within different market sectors, capital requirement, level of technology and other such factors affect the conditions for the formation and growth of small business (Storey, 1982). But, on the basis of our interviews, the experience of business proprietorship among women is also highly influenced by two sets of factors: first, their attachment to entrepreneurial ideals and, second, the extent to which they are prepared to accept conventionally defined male–female relationships.

By attachment to entrepreneurial ideals we are referring to a set of attitudes characterized by the following features.[5] First, a belief in economic self-advancement. Secondly, an adherence to individualism in terms of 'self-help', 'personal responsibility' and 'self-reliance'. Finally, strong support for the work ethic with profits and high living standards were seen as the just rewards for those who have made the necessary personal effort and sacrifices. The extent to which women proprietors are attached to these ideals varies considerably. While some are highly committed to profit-making, others prefer security and to exercise their technical, craft and professional skills often by foregoing higher profit margins. Such variations have important implications for the ways in which they run their businesses.

By acceptance of conventionally defined gender roles we refer to the extent to which women accept their subordination to men. Athough some women resent this, others willingly regard this as both 'morally' and 'naturally' correct. Because of their subordination, therefore, the social position of most women is determined by the men with whom, either by marriage or by the couple relationship, they are personally attached. Consequently, their economic circumstances and life-styles are acquired through men and they thereby acquire a vicarious identity (Finch, 1983). Thus, as far as female proprietors are concerned, there are important variations among them in the degree to which they are prepared to accept a vicarious identity. This, then, will affect their commitment to business growth and the priority they attach to their enterprises compared with other facets of their lives.

If, then, the attachment to entrepreneurial ideals and the acceptance of conventionally defined gender roles affect the behaviour of businesswomen it is possible to describe them in terms of the following typology (see Figure 4.1):

(1) *Conventional* women business owners are those who are

		Attachment to Conventional Gender Roles	
		High	*Low*
Attachment to	*High*	Conventional (1)	Innovative (2)
Entrepreneurial Ideals	*Low*	Domestic (3)	Radical (4)

Figure 4.1   *Types of female entrepreneur.*

both highly committed to entrepreneurial ideals and to conventional notions about gender roles. Such women are often confronted with conflicting pressures emanating from their businesses and from domestic-based personal relationships since most of them will tend to be married. They tend to start-up on the basis of skills acquired through performing traditional female roles. Thus, they are often proprietors of guest houses, secretarial and nursing agencies, restaurants, catering firms and hairdressing salons. Since the enterprise can impose upon the domestic roles of those proprietors who are married, there is a tendency for profit-making to be achieved through strict cost-effectiveness within stable no-growth businesses.

(2) *Innovative* proprietors are those women who are highly committed to entrepreneurial ideals but who reject prevailing notions of the female role. They are strongly motivated by the pursuit of profit and business growth. For them, business is a central life interest to the extent that all other personal relationships are regarded as secondary. Proprietorship offers them new personal identities. There is a tendency, therefore, for such women to be unmarried and to have few friends. They have often encountered male prejudices in the labour market. Many will have enjoyed a relatively high level of education and experienced upward mobility in large-scale organizations. At the same time, however, these same experiences will have made them aware of the obstacles confronting career women and, as a result, they attempt to fulfil their personal ambitions through entrepreneurship. Such women trade with technical skills which have been acquired within the educational and occupational systems rather than by

fulfilling traditional female roles. They tend to be found running businesses within the postwar growth areas of graduate female employment, namely, market research, advertising, public relations and publishing.

(3) *Domestic* traders are those who have only a limited commitment to entrepreneurial ideals but who are strongly attached to the traditional female role. There is a tendency for them to be married and for them to regard their businesses as secondary to their primary roles as mothers and wives. As such, proprietorship offers opportunities for non-monetary self-fulfilment and for personal autonomy within parameters delineated by their other obligations. In a similar manner as conventional proprietors they trade with a variety of traditional female skills. Examples of their business activities include arts and handicrafts, health foods, beauty care, dressmaking, and the manufacture of highly specialized products for the home. Because they attach importance to the exercise of their personal skills and to work satisfaction, profits and business growth are given a low priority. Consequently, they usually trade with customers on a regular long-term and small-scale basis. Since most of them tend to be married, their husbands are often used as 'negotiators' for obtaining credit and commercial expertise. But most important of all, this pattern of trading is characterized by its very small-scale nature and by the fact that it is circumscribed by the demands and obligations of the family system. Thus, these proprietors regard their businesses as secondary to other aspects of their lives.

(4) *Radical* proprietors have a low commitment to both entrepreneurial ideals and to conventional female roles. They are often university graduates who, with their various skills, have been confronted with male prejudices within large-scale organizations. At the same time, various other personal experiences have led them to query traditional assumptions about the position of women in society. Accordingly, business ownership is seen to offer a means whereby women can overcome their subordination. Their businesses are not geared to profits and any accumulated assets are used to further the longer-term interests of women. As such, these enterprises tend to be associated with the women's movement and to be in such diverse spheres as publishing, printing, craft trades, retailing, education and small-scale manufacture. Because of

strong ideological commitments, these proprietors regard their businesses as social as well as economic units. They provide a context within which feminists can form personal identities and life-styles free from the contaminating influences of men. Such enterprises, therefore, are often regarded as an alternative to marriage and the family. Further, the strong egalitarian ethos of the women's movement shapes the pattern of ownership on the basis of jointly owned partnerships and co-operatives within which there are no hierarchically organized work patterns. Business growth is not shaped by the profit motive but by the need to provide self-financing services for women.

There are, then, different types of female proprietor. The ways in which they run their businesses can be understood by reference to their commitment to profit-making and to the traditional female role. There are probably more conventional and domestic business owners than there are of the other types. However, the women's movement and the continuing limited career opportunities available to women have, in all probability, increased the numbers of 'innovative' and 'radical' proprietors. In the following four chapters we draw further on our interview data in order to illustrate more fully the similarities and contrasts between the experiences of the four types of women business owners. We begin with the innovators.

Notes: Chapter 4

1   The interviews were conducted by the authors and by Maxine Pollock and Mina Bowater for whose enthusiastic assistance we are grateful.

2   Readers of this book, and some of our previous work, may be encouraged to know that our present research, on the nature of managerial careers and life-styles, *will* allow us to incorporate quantitative as well as qualitative data analysis.

3   Within a capitalist economy this applies equally to co-ownerships as to more conventional forms of private enterprise.

4   The response may well be different, of course, amongst women whose business enterprises have failed. However, the practical problems of locating ex-proprietors makes comparison extremely difficult.

5   The terms 'entrepreneur' and 'entrepreneurial' are commonly used in a variety of ways. In our text we use the terms 'business owner', 'proprietor' and 'entrepreneur' as equivalents. However, women business owners vary in their attachment to 'entrepreneurial ideals' as we define them.

PART TWO

Some Contrasting Experiences

5

Business as Career: Innovative Entrepreneurs

Of all businesswomen, those who may be regarded as innovators probably attract the most attention. The media often highlight their achievements in order to demonstrate how women can be successful in an overwhelmingly man's world.[1] Indeed, such women are usually portrayed as possessing personal attributes normally associated with men: those, for instance, of assertiveness, determination and ambition. These are the characteristics which are strongly emphasized by many Conservative politicians as necessary for the regeneration of an entrepreneurial culture, and the return to economic prosperity and fuller employment (Conservative Central Office, 1979). If the great majority of the new entrepreneurs are men, there are according to popular debate a small number of women who are 'beating men at their own game' by the sheer exercise of will-power, determination and, often, ruthlessness. But how accurate is this frequently held view? In this chapter we describe the strategies pursued by those women who are highly committed to the entrepreneurial ideal but who query, or even reject, conventional assumptions about the position of women in society. We discuss their work experiences, life-styles and personal identities and assess their rewards and sacrifices.

The average age of the fifteen women that we interviewed was 44; the youngest being 31 and the oldest 71. Six were married and of these, four had children. Of the nine single women, six had never been married while three were divorced. Their businesses were mainly in the areas of advertising, publishing, market research, interior design, printing, software computing, accounting and financial consulting. All the women we interviewed had started their own businesses, the average age of which was eight years. The oldest had been operating for approximately twenty years and the most recent for less than a year. With the exception of three enterprises where annual turnover ranged between £2.5 million and

£4 million, the yearly average level of trading was £40,000. There was also considerable variation in the number of employees; of the fifteen businesses, thirteen had between one and twenty employees, while two of them each employed roughly 700 people.

In Chapter 4 we discussed some of the more general reasons why women start their own businesses; we now consider the more precise factors motivating those who may be described as innovators. The interviews suggest that one of the major reasons why these women had started their own businesses was because of limited career prospects in large-scale organizations. In other words, they regarded entrepreneurship as a means for obtaining economic and personal success because of the inability to fulfil ambitions within more conventional career structures. The overwhelming majority of the women were university graduates who had been employed in a variety of middle-management positions. They felt their career prospects were limited because of the existence of various gender-related prejudices (Ashridge Management College, 1980; Davidson and Cooper, 1983b). These had been strongly felt by three of the women and were the chief reason why they had started their own businesses.

I'm quite ambitious. I want to do various things with my life . . . But in my last job there was no future in it. I set up this business because I was fed up with people saying 'Are you thinking of getting married?' or 'Are you having a child?' I got sick to death of it. Never got anywhere. Well, I thought, I don't have to put up with this. Who needs to? If you set up something on your own, as long as you survive, you don't have to listen to that. I love not having all those office politics. I just get on with the work. (aged 32, single, 1 employee)

After I got married, I announced to the Board that I was going to have a baby . . . They refused to accept that I wanted to come back as managing director of their market research subsidiary. They brought in somebody over me, and demoted me to director even though I was back at work after two months . . . They would not accept that you can be a managing director as well as a working mother. This resistance and totally stupid attitude meant an important turning point for me. I felt desperately I could do it better . . . just as simple as that. I got fed up being employed. I wanted to be an employer. . . I wanted autonomy, to be able to run my own business. (aged 50, remarried, 700 employees)

I worked my way up through British publishing and became an assistant editor in a literary agency. . . I walked out of that agency which I worked for because they said I was no good. That gave me the incentive . . . I had to extend myself . . . I started my own agency . . . I knew I was every bit as bright and successful as my male contemporaries, many of whom are still stuck in their jobs . . . I just wanted to make money for myself. I was certain I could put my talents into developing my own business . . . I'm pretty creative and I'm very energetic. (aged 42, single, 3 employees)

These women are typical of those who opt out of careers in large corporations because they resent working for other people. In this they share a common motive with a large number of male proprietors who also start their own businesses because they are not prepared to adhere to the supervision and control of others (Scase and Goffee, 1982). This, together with a general resentment of being an employee for the purposes of making profits for owners and shareholders, is a major reason why both men and women start their own businesses. For some, such businesses provide a means for 'getting by' and obtaining a satisfactory standard of living through trading in the market. Thus, for them, business survival and market stability is their major concern (Bechhofer *et al.*, 1974a). But with the others, as with the innovators in our study, there is a long-term commitment to business growth as a means for acquiring an ever-increasing level of personal success. Despite their frustrated careers, the women we interviewed had not rejected the success goals of modern society or the values associated with the work ethic. On the contrary, entrepreneurship was seen by them to be an alternative route for achieving the same goals. Indeed, for some of them it was seen to offer a strategy whereby hard work and endeavour could be better rewarded. As a result, they were usually preoccupied with running their own businesses to the extent of sacrificing almost everything else. Their personal identities were almost entirely tied up with the success and failure of their businesses and in this they expressed some of the more extreme features of psychological immersion that is so typical of successful male entrepreneurs (Kets de Vries, 1977). Their commitment to business growth is illustrated by three of the respondents in the following way:

I'd like to make enough money out of it to do more ambitious projects . . . I want to expand. I'm planning to go into related areas like television production . . . I want to branch out of publishing . . . You've got to grow, otherwise you're more or less thinking of cottage industry level. You've got to expand. You've got to think on a higher level. (aged 32, single, 1 employee)

At the moment there are a lot of options open to the company because we have a good reputation, we have good profits and we have good cash flow. The profits allow you to consider acquisition or diversification and the fact that we've got cash means we are in a very powerful position to pick up businesses. So we've had a very serious look at whether we should be buying complementary types of companies . . . We've diversified geographically over the years and we're extending that. We've already got two subsidiaries overseas and we're opening up in Scotland soon . . . Training is a major diversification and we're going to do more and more consultancy. (aged 48, married, 700 employees)

We're in the middle of expanding at the moment. We've just opened in New York and we're moving to new offices here. This office is getting more people and more business is coming in all of the time. We've started a new service to work for advertising agencies as opposed to our own company which works purely for individual clients. So we've expanded quite a lot and the idea is to make sure that we create different profit centres . . . After that, I have a hankering to start a china shop as well, which I'll do one day, but that will be in my spare time. (aged 31, divorced, 19 employees)

These businesswomen are highly committed to achievement and this can be a source of stress since personal goals, through business growth, are never fulfilled. As soon as one set of goals are achieved, they are superseded by others (Mednik, Tangri and Hoffman, eds, 1975). This, in turn, has implications for the ways in which they order their personal priorities; the business always comes first and all other relationships and interests are subordinated to it. Such sentiments are reflected in the following statements:

I always want to go and do the next thing. There's always another ladder to climb . . . that's what life is all about . . . There's always another challenge, another thing to do. Money is part of it . . . but I get my biggest kick out of my career, and that's what I always want to be free enough to pursue . . . I work all the time. I have no other life. Most weekends I work without a break all day Saturday, all day Sunday, you grow into it. I'm not married and I live alone . . . if I got married, I wouldn't be able to put in so much time . . . In my head there is always another ladder to climb. A man once said to me 'You're the only woman I've ever met who has a spirit of adventure'. That's exactly it. Ambition seems to be a dirty word to women, but for me it's not . . . I wouldn't give it up even for Rhett Butler. What the hell would I do with my time? I get a hell of a kick from it. I probably get a bigger orgasm out of doing a million dollar deal than screwing some man! I'd much rather get a 150,000 commission than a good fuck. And why should I, as a woman, feel embarrassed about admitting that? Of course, that's more of a turn on than going to bed with somebody. (aged 42, single, 3 employees)

With the company growing, it's all hands to the deck at the moment and I'm a very important part of the company . . . My working day usually starts at around 8.30 a.m. . . . and I suppose it finishes at about 7p.m. The business is my life, very much. You get involved with clients, you have to go out to dinner with them and talk to them . . . It does, however, restrict you from seeing your own friends and family . . . A lot of women say they couldn't do it . . . but some are very interested in work and are determined to start on their own . . . But you just live it all the time. If you're reading the paper on Sunday, you will undoubtedly find some bit of news that has something to do with the company and so your brain automatically starts thinking about the business. (aged 31, divorced, 19 employees)

I'm a workaholic. I must have something to strive for . . . I need to work, really need to work in order to feel useful and get excited, and so on. I don't think anyone else would employ me. This is what happens to entrepreneurs, we become very difficult to employ in the conventional way . . . The reason why I remain sane is I don't think of it as work – I just enjoy it. I just think it's incredible that I should be paid for doing it. (aged 48, married, 700 employees)

Such a commitment to work and to business growth has consequences for the ways in which these women run their enterprises. They tend to rely upon personal control mechanisms and to avoid the use of formalized procedures within which there is a clear delineation of work tasks. Instead, they deliberately create flexible and broadly defined roles within which employees enjoy a considerable degree of autonomy in the performance of their work tasks. Thus, there is a heavy emphasis upon employee loyalty and the personal charisma of the proprietor as a source of company commitment. It provides a means whereby employees are highly motivated because of their close identification with the goals of the business. Consequently, it is unnecessary for there to be more formal or 'tight' supervisory systems since the owner's own drive and determination creates an organizational culture within which employees feel obliged to perform effectively (Scase and Goffee, 1983). As a result, such enterprises are characterized by the absence of rules and regulations, and of hierarchical relationships. Relations between employers and employees in such businesses can appropriately be described as 'egalitarian' or 'democratic' since all are expected to co-operate and do their utmost for the good of the common cause; namely, the attainment of the proprietor's objectives for the business (Goffee and Scase, 1982a). These features and the converse absence of formal, hierarchical and impersonal supervisory procedures are reflected in the following:

> We don't believe in a hierarchical structure but very much in a horizontal-type system . . . I believe very strongly that if somebody is very good at market research that we should invest in them as people and let them run their own sections. That's more or less what's happened so far. It's the best way to give people incentives. Our most recent acquisition is another market research company which is operated quite separately. People don't know about our ownership at all. They're just autonomous . . . that's the way I see it developing along the lines of small service operations . . . People tend to work in little teams, so you might have a director and two or three executives who are responsible for a group of clients. They set themselves targets and they are responsible for keeping within them and making a profit . . . So it's a small team approach . . . When we recruit, I look for personal qualities, their attitudes towards work. They have to be pretty informal and relaxed people with a sense of humour. We're not a rigid and inflexible organization. We have to know how much a person is going to work well with a small team. You can see why women do well in this. Women tend to be very good at interpersonal relationships . . . The last time I interviewed anyone . . . we talked nothing about work at all. I took it for granted that she was an able researcher . . . I

talked to her entirely about her political attitudes . . . and frankly I picked her on that basis. I felt that this was somebody that I could work with. I liked her attitude, that's all. Very unscientific, I am sure . . . but personal qualities, whether you can work with somebody, is the most important point. (aged 50, remarried, 700 employees)

My employees love their jobs because I involve them in everything. We have discussions about what we are going to do. I ask them what we should charge for the courses and why . . . and I say if you've got an idea, then draft it out. So we run it as a team. Therefore, once they come, they stay . . . I am certainly offering more than a male employer. I have to say this. I run it in a very personalized way. They come and say to me that they would like a day off and I say 'Right, fine. That's grand. Work it out between you.' I don't bother about it. They keep their own checks . . . They know what they are paid per hour, they put down their total at the end of the week and one of the girls pays it out. It's only when they've run it for three or four months that I have a look at the figures . . . I certainly don't think a man would be so sympathetic or sensitive to the day-to-day domestic needs of these people. They don't have to explain anything to me . . . they don't have to tell me a rigmarole to justify their leave . . . But they are supervised on results. If I find a mistake I can blow my top. I can be extraordinarily patient when a person is learning and then I have a break point. I think they know where they stand. So supervision as such doesn't come into it. It's example and we talk about standards a lot . . . In hiring, aspects of their personalities are very high on the list. They've got to have a basic knowledge, but really they've got to work in a very small space and be able to get on with each other, because it's a team effort. I can't have a 'that's not my job' attitude. Women have a greater degree of people sensitivity and men tend to have a greater degree of thing sensitivity. A generalization, but I think men tend to see things through facts and figures and women see things through people – what effect things will have on people. (aged 71, single, 8 employees)

Somebody has described me as the company conscience. An awful lot of things don't even come to a management meeting let alone the Board because long before it ever gets to that stage they are saying that I won't have it. They know what I'll take and what I won't take . . . We had a manager a couple of years ago who came in with a management style which was based on the concept of checking up on people and she really would never have succeeded in our organization. She eventually resigned because I think she recognized it, too. The organization does, in fact, run on trust; on the assumption that people are doing their best and that their best is good. That penetrates right the way through . . . Every now and again some-body will take us for a ride but it's not very often. It's amazing what people can do and the energy and emotional hassle that you can save if you work on the assumption that it's a team . . . and we just work together . . . With the ethos of the company at the moment, it's easy as a woman . . . that, in fact is an asset. A male in his position could not really understand what it's like. (aged 48, married, 700 employees)

It is clear from these comments that many women proprietors organize their businesses on the basis of trust: it is assumed that supervisory controls are largely unnecessary because employees are committed to the employer's goals and that they are keen to perform diligently and effectively (Fox, 1974). It is for this reason that many employees are attracted to work in small businesses, even if it means lower wages, because they can enjoy a greater degree of autonomy and, hence, a higher level of job satisfaction. Such a 'high trust' relationship has considerable advantages for proprietors since it enables them to limit their time on employee supervision and to devote more of their energies to commercial negotiation and to other aspects of their business. A 'high trust' organizational culture, then, has important economic advantages; not only does it enable the proprietor to save time on supervision but, also, to reduce the need to employ managers and other supervisors. The creation of good human relations and the culti-vation of an effective and creative company culture, therefore, are not entirely inspired by sentiments of altruism but also by the rational, economic motives of employers (Peters and Waterman, 1982).

Small firms, then, consist of relationships between personali-ties. As such, the compatibility of employees is at a premium and it is hardly surprising that proprietors attach just as much impor-tance to personal attributes as they do to technical competence when they are recruiting their staff. Indeed, this accounts largely for the alleged harmonious atmosphere of most small businesses; employers recruit employees according to the extent to which they seem likely to be prepared to accept the 'shared' goals of the business. There is no place for either disagreement or animosity both among employees and between employer and employees since this will disturb the organizational culture, employee commitment and, therefore, operating efficiency (Scase and Goffee, 1982). Thus, the selection of the appropriate personalities is crucial for the ways in which these women run their businesses. As two of them told us:

> They are managed in a very informal way. We all do everything . . . But if they want help they come to me . . . In recruiting, we look for attitude – willingness, cheerfulness, enthusiasm. I couldn't care less about their skills because they can always improve them. If they fit in, they're in . . . I think many men managers would have real trouble running it in a woman's style. My staff do respect me and we're fond of each other. We're friends . . . we're very relaxed. It's a very easy relationship. They're absolutely loyal. Marvellous. We've been through a very sticky passage on the way here and they were marvellous. They worked long hours and they put up with temporary accommodation. They were very good. It works both ways. One girl here has two very young children and she knows she's only got to say she's got to go home and look after them and I let her. I do make special concessions but I don't feel that anybody takes advantages . . . they're good girls and they don't take advantages. (aged 52, divorced, 6 employees)

> We supervise fairly loosely. Being so small you've really got to get on with these people or else it is going to be very unpleasant all around. So we're trying to build up an atmosphere of mutual trust and loyalty – very much a family affair. For instance, when we took on our employees, we decided to take them all out for a meal to get to know each other socially. I couldn't come the heavy hand, quite honestly. I would be embarrassed about it. You get more out of people by being nice to them. (aged 35, divorced, 3 employees)

These businesswomen, then, supervise staff by exercising personal skills rather than by using more formal systems of control. A number claimed that in doing this it was an advantage to be a woman. We found this somewhat surprising in view of the claims by some writers that women face particular difficulties as managers, if only because they lack the necessary attributes of assertiveness which are normally regarded as necessary for effective management and which are usually acquired through male socialization (Larwood and Wood, 1977; Place, 1979; Davidson and Cooper, 1983a). The women we interviewed felt that, on the contrary, the use of 'female qualities', such as 'understanding', 'warmth' and 'caring', were more appropriate for supervising and motivating staff and, as a result, they were more effective than men as managers. As three of them argued:

> I certainly have a feeling, and I can't put any reason on it at all, but I just know if something is not right . . . Usually it turns out that my female intuition is right . . . With the staffing problem – which is perhaps the biggest headache of all when you are running a company – it works much better to have a female rather than a male at the top, to be able to understand everybody. People in our company are aware that I'm much more sympathetic to their needs and to their requirements and their wants. (aged 31, divorced, 19 employees)

> Technically, I'm the boss, but we're all friends together . . . I recruit people who have, more or less, our approach to life . . . I think a woman employer knows that women employees have got to go home and cook . . . so if somebody wanted to work slightly irregular hours, I'd let them . . . I'm good to them and I expect them to be good to me. I think I understand things more perhaps than a male attitude. (aged 59, single, 5 employees)

> I think it's a great advantage to be a woman employer because, on the whole, one tends to be more sympathetic possibly and to understand people's problems. All these people who are married, they've got children, they've got jobs – some haven't got husbands – but I think I'm more sympathetic to their emotions. Both to men and to women . . . I don't bully them which I think a lot of men employers might do. (aged 51, married, 5 employees)

Although the use of such personal attributes can be highly functional to the operating efficiency of small firms they tend, paradoxically, to inhibit business growth. In a small firm, the dynamic of employer–employee relationship based upon trust and mutual respect maintains a relatively stable system. This can impede growth since expansion may challenge the pattern of relationships necessary for economic efficiency. Growth, then, is often regarded by proprietors as very risky since the employment relationship would then need to be established upon a more impersonal and formalized basis. At the same time, it would be necessary for the owners to delegate and to reduce the day-to-day control which they exercise over the activities of their businesses. There is a reluctance for most small business owners, whether men or women, to do this (Goffee and Scase, 1982b; Scase and Goffee, 1983). But, for many women, it is particularly difficult since they manage their firms by utilizing their various 'female' attributes.

If, however, the proprietors do regard themselves as effective managers, how do they cope as traders in the market? Do they confront prejudices about their credibility as business traders or are they accepted, particularly by men, on equal terms? According to our interviews, most of these innovators feel they have successfully overcome many gender-related prejudices. But there does seem to be a contradiction in their attitudes towards negotiating with men. On the one hand, they argue it makes no difference they are women and that they are generally regarded by men simply as business proprietors. But, on the other, they often explicitly use their 'female' attributes for the purposes of gaining business advantages (Cooper and Davidson, 1982). Thus, many of them behave according to male-defined 'rules of the game' and because this is a strategy which can be used for achieving business objectives, it is hardly surprising that many of them prefer to negotiate deals with men. In negotiations with women, by contrast, 'femininity' cannot be used to the same advantage. The following comments are illustrative:

Let's take my role with clients. The curious thing about treating men with respect, which was drummed into me at home . . . is it's so innate in my personality . . . my clients always take me out to lunch . . . businessmen are lonely in a deep sense. The only thing that really turns them on is themselves and their jobs . . . I consider them to be absolutely fascinating and I love getting men talking about their jobs . . . I don't know many businesswomen, quite honestly. The few I meet, I think I get on badly with . . . I don't ever, as a woman, want to band together with other women . . . Almost certainly we're both 'prima-donna-ish'. I can see through her tricks as easily as that and probably she can see through mine. I don't really enjoy having women clients. I try to avoid it . . . What they don't realize is that their techniques over the years have been directed towards getting their own way with men. That's what women are good at . . . We don't live in an emancipated world at all at the level that I'm in. And that's what women should do, they should go out and get their own way with men. They shouldn't really try and get their own way with me. (aged 46, married, 11 employees)

Being a woman in a man's world – and as I said I'm not into women's lib – I find that I have plenty of help. It's a great advantage over some of my male colleagues . . . You get to a factory site, they take one look at you, they think, 'Oh gosh', and they all carry your cameras, they all help you empty your car. There's always someone who will always run around and help you . . . I don't go along with the butch woman thing and I don't say no . . . when someone wants to carry my camera . . . If you look all right, then that's fine and I find that I get a better deal . . . It's because I'm a woman – they don't see many women around and so they like to come along and chat me up . . . and you get a better deal. (aged 31, married, 1 employee)

One thing is very important to stress; if you're a female, retain your femininity. Say 'OK I can run this business but I'm also a female' . . . I wouldn't like to be thought of as a man running the business. I'm a female and you can actually use your femininity to get certain things. That sounds really nasty, but it has its uses on certain occasions . . . There's a slight element of 'the helpless female' . . . You've got to be careful in the way you dress . . . I dress fairly staidly, but still looking feminine, hopefully. (aged 32, single, 1 employee)

You can certainly use your feminine charm. I've never been very good with the feminine wiles, if I were, I would probably have married a millionaire. But feminine charm counts for a lot. It's always easier for a woman to get to see a man with a job than for a man . . . Often, I'll prefer to deal with a man than a woman. I'm much more wary if I'm dealing with a woman . . . I can't chat her up . . . Often in business, people like to deal with members of the opposite sex because at least it's someone other than their husband or wife, or boyfriend or girlfriend. (aged 35, married, 3 employees)

These, then, are some of the distinctive features associated with the ways these women behave as proprietors. What are the implications for their domestic, personal and social lives? It is, of course, necessary to distinguish between married and single women. For married women, domestic and business activities often create conflicting demands and generate many personal problems, while for single women marriage and entrepreneurship are usually perceived to be incompatible. Among managerial and professional women, there is a lower rate of marriage than among females as a whole (Cooper and Davidson, 1982; Korn Ferry International, 1982) and in the present study the proportion of unmarried proprietors was high. Some of these had explicitly chosen to start their own businesses in preference to getting married. There were others who felt that, for one reason or another, they were unlikely to get married and so, instead, had decided to devote their energies to business start-up. But there were also others who, having started their businesses, found that they had insufficient time to become involved in personal relationships. The reluctance of single women in our study to get married is reflected in the following.

> Marriage? I just think it is not right for me. I never fancied the idea. I just can't see what the big attraction is, quite honestly. I can understand why certain women are conditioned into believing that it is their goal in life to get married and to have children. But I can't understand why they can't see what their life is going to be like . . . never really fulfilling themselves . . . Where men give as good as they take, people can have lasting good relationships. But most men take more than they give, most women give more than they take. That's why they end up doing all the dogsbodying and men get all the glory . . . I'm happy because I'm achieving the things that I want to achieve and I think that life is about achievement. That's the satisfaction in life. It might only be finishing 50,000 sheets of paper, but when you've achieved it, you've done something. Sitting at home all day long, watching kids crawling around and talking baby language, how can any intelligent woman find that rewarding? (aged 31, single, 7 employees)

> The reason I didn't get married was that I didn't meet the people with whom I could work out the kind of life I wanted. I knew I wasn't ever going to be a slave wife and it was no good embarking on it . . . I would have had to forfeit my work . . . to pay attention to domestic duties . . . but it would have submerged me. I wanted to be a partner in the true sense of that word – I didn't want to be an appendage. I had sufficient foresight to see that most men, whatever they say, weren't really looking for what I was looking for. So I thought, no, not for me. (aged 71, single, 8 employees)

Perhaps such attitudes should not be regarded as entirely surprising in view of the importance which these women attach to the
qualities of independence and self-help for business start-up.
These, of course, are exactly the same attributes that are likely to
make marriage unappealing because of its connotations with
women's dependence and subordination. Further, they become
almost entirely preoccupied with their businesses, investigating
much emotional and psychological energy, but they neglect their
friends and other personal relationships. Consequently, their business immersion leads to personal isolation and, often, to feelings of
loneliness.

Without doubt, marriage is generally seen as a hindrance to
business success, a striking contrast to the attitudes of businessmen who generally feel that marriage and the unpaid labour of
their wives is vital for successful start-up. The conflicts between
marriage and running a business were clearly recognized by many
of the women we interviewed.

> The business is more than a career, it's a life-style. But I must admit
> I'm now beginning to change because I'm getting married. This has
> all happened in the last few months and it's changing my outlook. I
> think you don't want to be as devoted to the business as you have
> been before because you haven't got the time. You've got to spend
> time with your husband, it's as simple as that, really. There are
> going to be problems . . . I don't actually see how anyone can have a
> business like this – which is very, very demanding – and be a
> housewife. It must be impossible if you've got children . . . this is
> really why I want to cut back . . . so that I can have at least a fairly
> normal social life with my husband. (aged 43, single, 1 employee)

> I recently got married. Now people are walking in and saying to me
> 'How are you getting on in your new job; How's the cooking'? They
> sincerely believe that I go rushing home every night while my
> husband's sitting with his feet up. I can't understand it. The
> number of people who've asked me that, in all sincerity. Men as well
> as women! In my husband's office, they all have wives who look after
> them – wash their shirts and things. Their wives don't work, so it's
> not very easy for my husband. Poor guy, he wants to share every-
> thing but he doesn't want people to think he's an old softie. (aged
> 35, married, 3 employees)

Perhaps my husband didn't realize when we got married what I was like. I wasn't working on my own then, but for another company. But I was ambitious to be successful . . . I wanted my work to be recognized for what it was . . . I do see a conflict between my business and having children . . . I enjoy my work too much. I'm very hesitant to give it up . . . my husband would very much like kids . . . I think that's going to blow up one day. It's a bit sad actually, because I realize it's going to be a problem. (aged 31, married, 1 employee)

For some women, the conflicting demands become excessive; they recognize a choice has to be made – either the husband or the business. Often the business wins.[2] As one of the divorced proprietors told us:

My husband was very uncooperative . . . he expected me to do everything or be responsible for everything . . . I was responsible for all the housework . . . he and I were totally competitive . . . we had the same sort of jobs. It was impossible. Neither of us could stand the competition . . . it was a bit of a compromise all the way down the line . . . not as good a mother as I would like to have been, not as good a businesswoman, not as good a wife. (aged 50, remarried, 700 employees)

But there are further implications for their life-styles. Although the total priority which they give to their businesses is a factor which reduces their involvement in leisure activities, their loneliness is further reinforced by their business-owner identity. As with female managers, they often perceive that others, both men and women, regard them as 'strange', 'odd', and 'unusual' (Cooper and Davidson, 1982) if only because they are businesswomen. This, in turn, encourages them to devote even more time and energy to their businesses. Furthermore, they often regard other women, particularly those who are housewives with children, as boring and uninteresting. They usually have little respect for these women because they regard them as lacking in personal initiative in their economic dependence upon husbands. Consequently, they feel both estranged from men who, they think, regard businesswomen as 'odd' and from other women with whom they share little common interest. These points are illustrated in the following:

I think very often that men are very much afraid of the woman executive . . . I can talk to people but I don't think the relationship goes further than that – you know? It's a long time since I tried it but I think that if I wanted to get romantically involved with somebody, it might be very difficult to get over the barrier of 'Oh, my god! She's got a business of her own'. They recognize your *independence*, that you're not going to lean over and say, 'Please help me'. Most men feel they want heirs and dependants, don't they? . . . Men look for an element of dependence . . . when it's missing and you're meeting on equal terms, it's difficult for them to cope with . . . Yet, I don't feel unfeminine . . . But I think it would be very hard for me now to be very interested in trivia. I see women on the train reading things like *Woman's Realm* . . . I'm not really interested in what goes into women's magazines. I don't think I'm very interested in the gossiping about families and what my grandchild did and what my daughter did, and all the rest of it. (aged 52, divorced, 6 employees)

Increasingly, my friends are drawn from professional or businesswomen rather than housewives in Wimbledon. It's happened over the years, I've seen a change take place . . . Recently, I went to a college reunion . . . I probably have more in common with the women I met there than with women living in my immediate neighbourhood – in terms of attitudes and work ambitions. I never thought I would say that, but it's true . . . [But] men denigrate my achievements, if anything. One occasionally meets the very chauvinistic male who just won't accept it . . . There is the sort of Englishman who would sneer at a woman running a business . . . It's just an automatic traditional attitude. (aged 50, remarried, 700 employees)

People show themselves in a different light when you run a business. Men are actually frightened of you, that's what fascinates me . . . You think, 'Good god, what am I? An ogre?' . . . Most men like to dominate the woman in their lives. Men are just not used to women being independent – that's the thing they always mention. (aged 32, single, 1 employee)

Business ownership, therefore, isolates women to a greater extent than men, if only because they can be regarded by others as different and unusual. Consequently, they often face greater difficulties in establishing close personal relationships and in belonging to groups of friends. Further, because there are so few of them, female proprietors, like female managers, lack appropriate role models (Kanter, 1977; Cooper and Davidson, 1982) and with the absence of relevant support systems, they have little alternative but to imitate the behaviour of businessmen. It is, then, not surprising that many feel their major weakness as business owners is lack of toughness, assertion and those attributes normally associated with the popular ideal of the male proprietor. This can lead to real contradictions since they also recognize the business advantages of various 'female' attributes for the purposes of managing and motivating staff, and for negotiating with clients. As three of them claimed:

> In order to be taken seriously you've got to be tougher than you would normally. You've got to be really firm – particularly as I don't look fierce. You've got to let them know that you mean business. That I find difficult to do. I'd far rather use the gentle approach, but maybe that's wrong . . . If you're going to be a woman in business, you've got to be a certain type of person. You've got to be pretty strong and pretty tough to be able to cope. (aged 35, married, 3 employees)

> I'm far too nice – by which I mean I'm not really tough enough with people . . . [To succeed] women have to be very self-disciplined and determined. They shouldn't think that they can't do it when somebody says no . . . They shouldn't give in – but battle away and in the end you usually get there. (aged 51, married, 5 employees)

> Why are there so few businesswomen? I think it is this fear of risk-taking – perhaps a lack of what I would call creative thinking. This business of being afraid of falling over is something which is deeply offensive and hurtful . . . It is psychologically suggested that the whole concept of women's role is one of nurturing and, therefore, it's not risk-taking. But I don't agree with that. You look at the women who explored the West in America – they couldn't have been more caring mothers, but, by golly, they had guts. (aged 71, single, 8 employees)

These women, then, recognize the need to combine various 'female' and 'male' attributes if they are to be successful business owners; for example, sympathy, care and understanding needs to be combined with toughness and assertiveness.[3] But if businessmen do offer them a partial role model, it is not strange that they should find the women's movement unappealing. There seems two major reasons for this. First, they are strongly committed to ideals of individualism and, as such, stress the values of self-reliance and personal effort. Secondly, despite the awareness among many of them of the general subordination of women they strongly feel that this can be overcome through individual rather than collective effort. Thus, they reject the need for a feminist political programme which exclusively pursues the interests of women in general. It is, in this sense, that they argue self-help in general and entrepreneurship, in particular, offers opportunities for both men and women. Accordingly, they claim that government policies should be geared to improving the conditions for business start-up in general rather than orientated to the specific problems of women. In this sense, they feel that business ownership erodes differences between men and women because both are equal in taking risks in an impersonal market for profit.

The following statements illustrate their negative attitudes towards the women's movement and the general feeling that feminist policies are irrelevant for tackling the problems of women.

I don't like too much distinction between men and women . . . The opportunities are there for women just as much as they are for men. I think women make too much of it really. You should just get on with it and try to ignore it. The more women point to the differences, the more it's obvious that there's a difference . . . I don't like to see people pushing women's causes because that just draws attention to it and makes people think that they are different – inferior. The way for women to gain acceptance is just to get on with it and show them that you can be as good as a man. (aged 35, divorced, 3 employees)

At times, the women's movement makes me very angry. Everyone has been given a brain and it's up to you to use it the best way you can. There are undoubtedly restrictions for females and those we have to break, but if you're really determined, if you really want to go about it, you can break them. You can get through them. You don't have that many problems if you really want to do it . . . Women can become terribly dictatorial in trying to force other women who are actually happy to do something they don't want to do . . . I have tremendous admiration for Maggie Thatcher . . . she's come up with a philosophy that she is going to make work and she's stuck to her guns. Whether she's right or wrong, she's staying there. (aged 31, divorced, 19 employees)

I don't believe in helping women just because they are women – poor dears, they need help! You've still got to prove yourself as a *person*. Basically, if you can run a business well, it doesn't matter whether you are male or female. It's very bad – men get very aggravated and start fighting back. I don't want them to think I'm in business just because the government helped me. (aged 32, single, 1 employee)

Why should women be singled out? I think there should be special arrangements for child care . . . but as to whether women business owners should be helped out – no, I don't think so. Men have got to fight it out on their own, why shouldn't the women? As long as there isn't prejudice . . . women shouldn't have any preference over men. Poor men! (aged 35, married, 3 employees)

As a businesswoman, I think that any policies which are in favour of the small company are a very good move. It's very important that we get back to realizing that the small company initiative is very significant . . . But some of the legislation is too altruistic and it makes it impossible for small companies to survive. One of the examples is the maternity legislation. As it was originally couched, that was absolute nonsense . . . How can you keep jobs open in a tiny organization? . . . [As for women business owners] there aren't all that many so I don't know that there's any point in making a particular category. (aged 71, single, 8 employees)

In conclusion, it seems that these businesswomen whom we describe as innovators subscribe to many of those attitudes popularly associated with the 'classical' male entrepreneur (McClelland, 1961; Kets de Vries, 1977). Generally speaking, they have opted out of careers as managers and professional employees in order to pursue material success and personal autonomy through proprietorship. In doing this, they are prepared to sacrifice personal relationships and to exploit conventional notions of femininity for their own business ends. These innovators, however, represent but one type of businesswoman – those who are highly committed to profits and who reject the traditional female role. We now turn our attention to those proprietors who, in different trading circumstances, exhibit contrasting attitudes and behaviour to these women.

Notes: Chapter 5

1   During the research several national newspapers and popular women's magazines ran features and, in some cases, major competitions which were directed primarily towards the innovative entrepreneur.
2   In our view, the complex relationship between proprietorship and (1) marriage (or an equivalent couple relationship), (2) domestic duties (3) child-bearing and child-rearing and (4) other 'family responsibilities' for innovators, and other women business owners, is worthy of further detailed research.
3   Such a strategy may be illustrative of the androgynous concept (whereby masculine and feminine personality traits and behaviours are combined) as discussed by Kinzer (1980).

6

Persisting Patterns: Conventional Businesswomen

There have always been women who have started their own businesses. There is, for instance, a very large number of women who own hairdressing salons, guest houses, secretarial and nursing agencies, health-care and keep-fit businesses, retail corner shops, and so on (Goffee, Scase and Pollack, 1982). Some of these women are self-employed with no employees but there are those who engage a limited number of staff. There is a strong tendency for many of these women to be highly committed to entrepreneurship but, unlike the innovators we discussed in the previous chapter, they are also strongly attached to the conventional female role. How then, do such women run their businesses and with what consequences for their self-identities and life-styles?

In our study we interviewed fourteen women of this kind who owned a variety of businesses, including office-cleaning, secretarial, clerical and employment agencies, retail shops and guest houses. All had started their own businesses which, on average, had been trading for about seven years; the longest had been established for nineteen years and the most recent for two years. Annual turnover, except for one enterprise which exceeded £3 million ranged between £25,000 and £140,000. The number of employees ranged from one to twelve with the exception of two businesses, one of which employed 80 people and the other 950.

The average age of these businesswomen was 45 with the youngest being 30 and the oldest, 68. Of the fourteen, one was divorced, two were widowed, two had never married and nine were married or cohabiting at the time of the interview. Ten of the women had children. By comparison with the innovators, more of these conventional proprietors were married with children; indeed, this had an important bearing upon the reasons why they had started their own businesses.

Compared with the women we discussed in the last chapter, these owners were less likely to have been previously employed in large-scale organizations. They had not been in career jobs and confronted with restricted prospects for promotion. Unlike many of the innovators we interviewed, therefore, resentment about limited career prospects was rarely a motive for business start-up. None of them had enjoyed long-term and secure employment and not one of them possessed higher educational or professional qualifications. Before starting their own businesses, most of them could best be described as 'secondary' workers (see Chapter 2) who had moved in and out of the labour market depending upon employment prospects and according to their various domestic and family commitments.

Whereas the innovators had deliberately decided to start their own businesses in order to develop their talents and skills removed from the prejudices and controls which they experienced as employees, the conventional businesswomen were more likely to set up enterprises out of sheer economic necessity; primarily for the purposes of supplementing a low family income. Among the married women we interviewed, for example, this was often very low because of the husband's unemployment, ill-health, level of wages, or short-time working.[1] Indeed, these women were essentially 'working class' in terms of being married to husbands with less-secure, poorly paid jobs. Business start-up for them has to be understood in these terms; they were driven by the need to earn money rather than by the search for greater personal autonomy and self-satisfaction. The way in which economic necessity forced these women to start their own businesses is illustrated in the following remarks.

I started because my husband left me. I had a three-week-old baby and I needed to work so I took in typing . . . to enable me to look after her. Gradually I got the idea of opening a small office to enable me to take in typing. Then I decided to go into other things – sending out temps. It was a case of economic necessity rather than grand dreams of fame and fortune. At the time I had only misery and heartache, wondering how on earth I could bring up my baby to the best of my ability. (aged 68, remarried, 950 employees)

I needed money. My husband was a farm worker . . . he was on a wage of about £10 a week {some twenty years ago} with a free house. My husband was an alcoholic . . . he'd been to sea and he was an alcoholic.

He was on and off all our married life. He suffered various bouts. He
died of alcoholism. His early capacity was always limited. He would
get a job then go off on a binge for two or three weeks and lose the
job. We were in twenty-one houses in nineteen years. Every time he
lost his job, we lost the house and had to move again. So that gave
me quite a bit of practice at being self-reliant and strong . . . My
earnings were never pin money, they were needed to feed us . . . We
never went hungry but there was never any money left for anything.
Finally, we lost the house – and he wasn't going to be able to work
much longer anyway because he was getting on towards 60 . . . If I
had had the choice, I'd never been in the retail trade at all. I only did
it because I had to get the money. I'd have liked to write. I always
wanted to write. (aged 60, widowed, 4 employees)

It really wasn't my intention to run my own business . . . My
husband was always telling me how short of money we were . . . I
felt I wanted to help boost our income with additional income . . . I
just realized that this was a very good business to be in and I had a lot
of contacts by that time and I thought I could do it by myself . . .
But if I had chosen I wouldn't be in this business because I don't like
the business – it doesn't interest me whatsoever. The actual business
is not creative and I came into it by a fluke really . . . In fact I
wanted to have a gardening centre. (aged 53, married, 80
employees)

These motives for business start-up are in sharp contrast to those
discussed in the previous chapter; there is no positive commitment
to business ownership in the sense of it being related to a need for
high achievement and a search for self-fulfilment. On the contrary,
the motive is to make money to make ends meet. This, in turn, has
important repercussions for the ways they run their businesses.
Although they are committed to making profits, they are not
geared to business growth. Instead, they are usually preoccupied
with maintaining a level of trading within market niches with a
minimum degree of competition and uncertainty.[2] How is this
compatible with a strong commitment to profit-making? Unlike
innovators who strive to optimize their profits through growth,
this group of conventional businesswomen are primarily concerned
with maintaining their profits by keeping overheads, wages and all
other costs to an absolute minimum. This can lead to a tendency
for them to exploit other women who tend to be unskilled second-

ary-sector employees. They do this by a number of means, from using unregistered part-time employees to relying heavily upon subcontracted home or outworkers. Thus, these women owners' commitment to profit and their gearing to business stability often leads to the employment of low-paid, lesser-skilled women in the labour market. The lack of a commitment to a personal achievement through business growth is evident in the following remarks.

> I'm not a tycoon type, like Marjorie Hurst. She's ambitious and I'm not. I want the satisfaction of doing things and then finishing them off. She wants to build an empire, and I don't. I really would hate to be a millionaire. I don't want to have so much that things are not enjoyable any more . . . You can only wear one dress at a time and drive one car at a time, let's face it . . . We live, we don't need to borrow and we have a fair salary from it, but a person can only do a certain amount in a day. Possibly, if we really wanted to build it up we could advertise, get in more staff, get a word processor in, and do all that. To do that we'd have to put a lot more money into it, for a start. (aged 51, widowed, self-employed)

> People who advise me say, 'You must have other shops because you've got the formula right and it's good. But all I can see, if I did, is me sitting in my car rushing between each shop, making sure everything was how I wanted it. Because the whole point about this shop is it is very personal. OK, maybe I could have another one . . . But I just know how exhausting it is and how tiring it is, and how it is totally on my back. Nobody else worries at the end of the day, nobody else is going to take any of the pressure off me. Nobody cares – of course they don't. It's my business . . . I'm totally responsible and it's really a matter of knowing how much I can cope with. I don't want to over-work myself and then let my marriage and my family suffer. (aged 32, married, 4 employees)

Often, the use of cheap female labour is justified by reference to competition and the operation of market forces. It is further legitimated by the claim that they are giving work to women who would otherwise be unemployed. These business owners often argue that they are powerless in the face of market forces to improve the wage rates of their employees since to do so would merely damage their trading position, undermine the profitability of their enterprises and restrict the extent to which they can provide jobs. As two of them stated:

I feel so sorry for some of the ladies. That sounds terrible but it's just that most cleaners work terribly hard, they really do. Particularly those women that have got five or six children, who keep their homes running and yet have other little jobs. I find it terribly disturbing that they work so hard . . . They have so many problems, most of them. They have a lot of children, they have a lot of responsibilities and they don't have a lot of money. Some of them will do anything just to keep out of the home. They have husbands who beat them up or whatever . . . [But] I'm not so soft as I used to be. When I first started, I was terribly naïve. I've always been a socialist and I had tremendously high socialist ideals. Unfortunately, I've been terribly disillusioned because I find that the more you give people the more they take advantage. For example, when I first started, I would always pay everybody for sick pay . . . Then I found that I wasn't getting half the staff in any more – they were always sick . . . So I put a stop to sick money completely, unless I know they're really sick . . . That's the only way to stop absenteeism. It makes me sad that it should be like that. But if you are very polite and nice to people they think you're soft, there's no doubt about it . . . Actually my sympathies are with the staff far more than they are with the business owners. The people who work for me are low paid and I'm always striving to get more money for them because I think they deserve it. But you have to have a wage structure that enables you to get quotations on new jobs. I pay quite well (the basic rate is £1.65 an hour) but not as much as I would like to. They are the lowest of the low as far as wages are concerned and I find that very difficult to handle. [But] they couldn't get more working for anybody else. The market determines the going rate. (aged 53, married, 80 employees)

We have people on a subcontracted basis to do manufacturing. I have a whole troupe of outworkers and established dress factories who produce the clothes for me, but they're not employed by me. They are paid by cheques and cash, depending on the amounts . . . I find it extremely difficult morally dealing with individual outworkers because these people are paid abominably. It's hard for me to morally accept it even though the people who work for me end up with two or three times the amount that somebody else would earn elsewhere. I have a lot of embarrassment about paying them. It's not something I could cope with easily. It's something I've got used to . . . They are women stuck at home – working-class women at home with children, a greater percentage of them Asian . . . [As a child] I hated the idea of business. I could never morally accept it. To me it meant that people were cut-throat and evil. It represented all the bad things in people. I never accepted there was any other way until a year ago when we were faced with bankruptcy. I realized I had to change my principles and that brought me face to face with a lot of things about myself that I would rather not know . . . I find myself now having fallen entirely into my own trap – into the principles and philosophies I despised all my life. I find myself actually adhering to them because they are beneficial to the business. (aged 31, single, 10 employees)

By comparison with male employers, these women are often more aware of the problems encountered by low-paid employees. This is probably because they themselves, before starting their own businesses, are more likely to have received low wages and to appreciate the problems that women face when looking after children on a limited income. Indeed, the nature of their enterprises normally means that these business owners employ a different quality of staff compared to innovators. If the latter, because of their trading activities tend to employ more highly skilled employees on a more-or-less permanent and full-time basis, conventional proprietors, as we have suggested, usually make use of cheap, unskilled women as outworkers or part-timers. This, in turn, has implications for their style of leadership; if innovators adopt an egalitarian strategy and explicitly cultivate a high-trust culture, these conventional businesswomen use a tactic which can be described as maternalist. In many ways, it is analogous with the paternalism used by many male proprietors of small firms (Scase and Goffee, 1982). It rests upon the cultivation of a close personal relationship between employer and employee within a framework of mutual obligation in which proprietors emphasize the common objectives of both employer and employee while, at the same time, maintaining a degree of social distance (Newby *et al.*, 1978). It is this greater emphasis upon hierarchical authority which separates the maternalist supervisory style from the more egalitarian manner favoured by the innovators. Indeed, the ability to establish a close working relationship with employees while maintaining traditional employer prerogatives requires a delicate balance. Employers must be neither too close to, nor too remote from, their employees and they must be able to sympathize with them while, at the same time, preserving the right to act in the best interests of the business. Proprietors normally obtain these skills through the experience of running their own businesses, coupled with knowledge about the workers' point of view derived from their own previous background as low-paid employees (Goffee and Scase, 1982a). But problems often arise when they become too emotionally involved in their employees' personal problems. This can divert their time and energy from running the business, threaten the social distance they maintain and, hence, their authority as proprietors. By becoming too friendly or familiar with their staff they may be unable to take difficult but necessary and economically rational decisions. They cannot, however, become too distant from their employees for two major reasons. First, to do so would undermine the personal nature of the employer relationship. It is this which often encourages employees to work flexibly within a rudimentary or even non-existent division of work tasks (Scase and Goffee, 1983). Secondly, it can jeopardize what many women proprietors feel to be their major strength as employers: their ability to understand employees', and particularly women's, personal problems. The essential nature of the employment relationship in these small businesses was aptly summed up by one of the proprietors.

> First and foremost it's your own business. It's *you – your* character, your personality, which makes it . . . In the last count *I'm* going to tell someone what to do but really it isn't a 'them and us' scene. I mean, we all have drinks together after work . . . so it's like a little family business. People are terribly pretentious to treat small companies like ICI. Obviously, if you get bigger you're not going to have so much to do with people. But if you're working in a small area of space you are. You can't pretend you're a managing director. You know you can't pretend you're a manager of IBM when you're not. (aged 30, single, 7 employees)

But how are close employer–employee relationships established in such a way that they do not challenge the proprietor's prerogatives? Primarily, a crucial aspect of the maternalist strategy is to define the business as a family within which strong parallels are drawn between employers and employees and between mothers and children. This enables these businesswomen to maintain their authority while, at the same time, to arbitrarily reward and punish. These themes are illustrated in the following:

I've very friendly with all of my employees . . . I feel we have a very good relationship and that is vital. I know about their outside problems. I do try to ask them about their lives all the time . . . [But] funnily enough, I almost have to make myself be more removed. That's something I've had to learn. I've been too friendly, I think. Naïvely at the beginning – one doesn't want to fall out with anyone. But I have learned that I have to be tougher and firmer about certain things. It's very difficult to learn to be firm yet friendly, to be fair yet very firm. I've had experience with girls who pushed me to the limit to see how far they could go . . . You must get things very straight when you employ them and have it totally on paper – all that they're allowed, everything – and stick rigidly to it. Then, when they've been wonderful I spoil them. But I have to learn not to spoil them too much. It's a funny mistake in reverse. I think that's a feminine problem. I think women are very much like that. With children you reward them and say 'Well done', so much that you say 'Well done' to everybody for everything. It's overdoing it. I do feel some of my staff are like children in a sense. It's funny. Like children, some of them certainly have tried to take advantage of me – just to see how far they can go. But that's what children do. I learned that from my children so therefore I can see it . . . I hate anyone to be upset or miserable. It's so important that they're happy with the job – that they love it. That's the trouble. I want everyone to be happy, but to them it's just a job. I have to keep remembering that. (aged 32, married, 4 employees)

I'm much more objective now than in the early days . . . I'm told by most of my friends that I'm a much tougher lady than I was four years ago – that's because I've had to make some rotten decisions . . . In the early days I got terribly involved with employees, which was very wrong. I stand back a bit now. I'm very much the boss now. Not that I lord it over them at all, but I deliberately do not become close personal friends . . . It's best I don't become too friendly – although they certainly look upon me almost as a mother figure, if you like, and we get terribly involved sometimes . . . it's because we *are* a small company and there is more of a family atmosphere in a way. When the girls go out on jobs they're referred to as 'one of Pam's girls' . . . We have a dinner once a year . . . all the girls who temp for us on a long-term basis are invited at my expense . . . and I'm very much the mother figure sitting at the head of the table. I always give a small speech and a lot of them buy me gifts . . . The relationship started to change the minute I stopped temping myself and started to run the office. It wasn't all of my making. They immediately took a step back from me. I think it's just the pecking order. The British, in particular, are very much sticklers for this. Everybody knows their position in the pecking order – that's what it is. (aged 46, married, 2 employees)

I frequently feel that I get like a mother towards my staff. Sometimes they don't know it and sometimes they do. But if you're wise, you don't let them be too aware of it . . . It's not a deliberate strategy although I'm conscious of it happening. I think if you deal with people in a small business like this you've got to care rather than walk away from their problems. After all, they don't walk away from my problems . . . Once or twice a year I take them out for a meal and their husbands come too. We have a very good time. In a small office you get to know your staff and their problems and the things that worry them. But always within limits. I wouldn't have my staff back to the house to entertain. I tend to believe that once you leave your business, you leave your business and try to forget about them! (aged 44, divorced, 3 employees)

As these accounts illustrate, a key assumption underlying the maternalist strategy is that employers use their authority to act benignly in the interests of employees. Thus, the arbitrary decision-making of proprietors is perceived to be quite legitimate by employees since it is assumed that the outcomes will be to their advantage. In return for this benevolence, employees are expected to show commitment, loyalty and gratitude.[3] But such a response can never be assumed; it has to be cultivated and even among the unskilled and lower paid, some employees are seen to be more grateful than others. These tend to be older female workers whose opportunities in the labour market are, of course, highly limited (Webb, 1982). One of the businesswomen made the distinction in the following terms:

I've always found, over the years, that if you're nice with other people they don't mind what they do for you . . . one of the main things is to have people who are adaptable and don't mind how

much trouble they go to . . . but I found it very difficult employing
young people . . . To be perfectly honest, I found that they hadn't
one-quarter of the energy or enthusiasm. I always had to ask them to
do things. They'd never think of doing it. I know one girl used to
say to the others, 'I don't know why you bother – it's not your
business'. It's this sort of attitude . . . they come in, they're
yawning and they're half asleep. Everything's a big bore, with no
interest. I didn't want that . . . I've found that it's much better to
have women of middle age who are really pleased to work. Their
families have grown up and they're really pleased to have something
to do. They like the companionship of working. They seem to enjoy
it. (aged 52, married, 12 employees)

Of course, maternalism as an employer strategy relies heavily
upon the compatibility of personalities within the context of a
close face-to-face relationship. As one of the proprietors remarked:

When you're hiring people the most important criterion is that they
fit in. They've got to be *really* enthusiastic and *want* to do the job –
and they've got to sort of fit in with the company. I look for people
who make me feel good. If they make me feel nice, if I enjoy talking
to them, then they'll probably make customers feel the same. In the
end, you get a feel for it. I don't make so many mistakes any more.
(aged 33, cohabiting, 1 employee)

The recruitment of staff, therefore, requires the exercise of
intuition and personal judgement. In the secondary labour
market, within which most of these businesses operate, it is
possible for employers to pick and choose workers according to
their personal as well as their technical attributes. Accordingly,
many of these proprietors feel that, as women, they possess qualities of insight which many male proprietors lack. They believe that
female employers are better equipped to handle relationships with
their workers, particularly when these tend to be other women.
Two proprietors described these points in the following terms:

From my experience of work, women like working for women . . .
we have a lot more understanding of each other's needs. I've got two
younger women working for me and they've got a day in the month
when they're not feeling very well. I can usually spot it. I can usually
see what's wrong with them before they ever *say* what's wrong. They

don't have to come and say 'I'm not very well – can I go home?' I'll tell them to finish up early before that. You won't get a man doing that because he hasn't got the insight to know about it. That's only one example. But I do think, as a woman, that I can understand women better and see what they want better. (aged 60, widowed, 4 employees)

I think that if you're a woman and you're dealing with women, you must have a basis for understanding the problems of women. Men . . . are much harder than women. They're not as understanding of their employees . . . Generally, I can choose my employees quite well. I can read their characters fairly well. I'm intuitive about it . . . I like to deal with other women, I really do. (aged 53, married, 80 employees)

Many of these proprietors justify the use of lower-paid and easily replaceable home and part-time married women workers in terms of the peculiar problems which they face as a result of their domestic and family responsibilities. As such, many see themselves as providing a valuable service for their female employees because they are offering employment and wages in ways that are compatible with their 'rightful' roles as housewives and mothers. Two of the proprietors explained their use of female home and part-time workers in these terms:

I originally set up the business to find work for women who were unable to work a conventional office day. The majority of them were women who were tied at home with children . . . Some were widowed, separated, divorced, or unmarried mums. Others were married to non-financial supporting mates . . . money *had* to come in, and we found work for them. Not only to give them financial support, but also to help their self-respect – so that they didn't have to apply for social security. It's been so successful that quite a lot of them still prefer to work that way, although they could work outside the home if they wanted to . . . I believe that the mother should be at home for young children at certain times, where possible. Sometimes it isn't possible and this is why I tried to create a situation where mothers won't be separated from their children but can still earn themselves a fiver. I've had mums who would work overnight because it was the only time their children were quiet. But I knew they needed work – so we sort it out on a sociological basis. (aged 61, married, 3 employees)

I'm a very great believer in part-time workers. Not only because you don't have to pay them so much – obviously – but when you're feeling jaded, they're like a breath of fresh air. Every time they come in, it's like a whole new world to them. And it's terrific for the business. That's got to be true . . . I now realize how important their job is. They wouldn't in any way want a full-time job because their families are important to them. But it's a lifeline for them. It's a tremendous interest for them outside their four walls or whatever. And that's nice for me. I like that. (aged 35, married, 3 employees)

Although the maternalist strategy emphasizes the similarity of authority relationships within families and small firms, this only serves to conceal the more obvious dimensions of the cash nexus which ultimately binds the employment relationship. Thus, in the final analysis, these businesswomen are quite prepared to use their proprietorial authority to enforce employee compliance and to act in an autocratic manner. This, according to many of the women we interviewed, was necessary for calculative, economic decision-making and for operating efficiency. These points were stressed by two of the women.

We've had to sack a few people for turning against us. You have to watch that . . . Occasionally, you'll get a bad apple with a bit of influence who'll start turning against us, saying, 'They did this, they did that. I bet they're making a mint.' Things like that. The whole atmosphere can change . . . I don't find the dirty work difficult any more . . . We always felt we didn't like to hurt people. But in the end, you're really hurting them more by not being honest. And I've got a business to run. I'm not running a charity . . . We let people have their say . . . but we try to be practical . . . I'm sympathetic but we have got a business to run . . . In the beginning especially, people didn't take us seriously. The girls used to think . . . we didn't have much authority . . . [But] you've got to have some kind of authority. Your statements have got to carry some weight . . . It's a bit like teaching in a way. The more experience you get, the more authority and credibility you get. (aged 33, cohabiting, 1 employee)

It took me a long time to get the right employees. You weed out a lot. You kiss a lot of frogs before you get a prince! . . . I run the thing entirely, I'm the boss, no doubt about that. We have a very good democractic way of running the business. We have great discussions and then *I do what I want to do*. I've a completely autocratic idea of how to employ people. It's my business. I'm the one who is going to make or lose money, so whatever decisions get to be made, in the end they've got to be mine. I listen to their advice but at the end it's what I say that's got to go . . . We're not on Christian-name terms. I'm Mrs Forder and they are Shirley, Julia, whatever . . . and there's quite a division here between workers and management! (aged 60, widowed, 4 employees)

As with the egalitarian style adopted by innovators (see Chapter 5) maternalism can help to sustain harmonious working relationships but it can also be an impediment to business growth. Because of their lack of formal management skills, conventional businesswomen possess no other means for supervising staff and this restricts the likelihood of business growth which normally requires the use of more impersonal forms of control (Newby, 1977). Maternalism, therefore, maintains the essentially small-scale nature of female-owned businesses so that the small firm which does expand to any significant extent is an outstanding exception. Business stability, indeed, is the general feature of all small businesses, whether they are owned by women or men (Storey, 1982).

So far we have discussed the way in which these conventional proprietors run their businesses, but what are the effects of business ownership upon their life-styles, attitudes and behaviour? Generally speaking, they are committed to their families and to other personal relationships and, by contrast with the innovators, their businesses do not predominate to the almost total exclusion of everything else. If innovators decide *not* to get married because of the detrimental effects this will have on their businesses, conventional proprietors often start their own businesses *after* they have been married for some time and only when start-up will not challenge or destroy personal or family relationships. This is illustrated in the following comments:

In my case I've always had to run the business and family together. When we ran the kennels we lived on the premises and it's the same in this shop. The house and the business are together − you can't separate the two things. You are living with them together . . . I never got away from the domesticity and the business activity certainly wasn't a way of escape. I didn't think 'Oh, poor me, I'm only a housewife', because from a very early age I've always combined my housewife role with the business . . . I've always had my work and my house interacting. (aged 60, widowed, 4 employees)

I'm very lucky to have a business that is doing so well and that I can cope with *and* run my home. That's what women sometimes suffer from – not being able to do both . . . I am really strict with myself and say to myself that this comes last – this meaning the business . . . My children, really always come first because for women, children just do matter that much . . . I'm lucky that I have a good basic marriage. Possibly, I knock it and kick it but I think if I didn't have it I would have much more pressure in my life and would probably be worse at running the business. (aged 32, married, 4 employees)

I'm pleased that I didn't start in business when the children were younger. When I started, the youngest was about 15. I'm pleased that I spent those years at home with them. I don't regret that at all . . . I wouldn't have missed a family for anything . . . and I wouldn't like to have started the business when the children were young . . . [now] the family prefers it – that I've got this interest. When people are at home not doing anything they're apt to find they don't feel well, or start complaining about things. Whereas, if you've got an interest, the family actually prefers it. (aged 52, married, 12 employees)

Conventional proprietors, then, usually run their businesses in ways which are compatible with their domestic obligations. Accordingly, many of them only go into business after various family demands – for example, bringing up children – have declined. They usually start trading at an older age than innovators but the congruence between their business and domestic roles is reinforced by two further factors. First, the maternalist employer style is derived from the mother role and so domestic experiences are seen to be entirely relevant for running their businesses as 'families' according to the canons of 'good housekeeping'. Secondly, a fit between the demands of business and the home can be created using domestic facilities for business start-up. This then enables them to allocate their time to both the home and the business in a flexible manner. But what are the implications for husband–wife relationships?

For this group of women, business ownership does not seem to lead to a restructuring of conjugal roles. As wives, they continue to perform the traditional household tasks normally undertaken by women within working-class families (Clarke, 1979). Their businesses, therefore, are grafted upon these domestic duties. Consequently, a large number of them work extremely long hours which, for most, is regarded as acceptable because of their dual roles. Further, they rarely expect their husbands to be actively involved in the running of their enterprises and nor do they require them to undertake additional household tasks. As one of them with a more understanding husband stated:

> My husband is very understanding, very sympathetic . . . he knows that the business *is* important for my own happiness . . . [But] he works very long hours and doesn't get home before eight in the evening. So, as I'm at home in the morning, I do fit in a few chores with my business. If I'm tired or ill, he will always make me a cup of tea or cook me a meal if necessary. I can't really complain. He does as much as he can for the amount of time that he's here. I don't mind having a go at the decorating . . . but with electrical things he's much better . . . he looks after things when the heater or the washing machine go wrong. (aged 38, married, 1 employee)

But in general, the experiences of these businesswomen are in sharp contrast to those of male proprietors. During start-up there is a tendency for men to rely upon the unpaid services of their wives and to abdicate all of the domestic duties to them (Scase and Goffee, 1980b). However, if for women, proprietorship does not lead to a restructing of husband–wife roles, it is hardly suprising that it has few effects for their self-identities. Whereas innovators we interviewed were acutely aware of their atypicality and their social marginality, this group were not. They do not see themselves primarily as businesswomen and this is partly because of the ways in which their businesses are grafted on to other personal and family relationships, and partly because of the tendency for most of their clients and employees to be women. Proprietorship, accordingly, does not query their gender-based identities. As one of them argued:

In my business, the asset is that I'm in the right business for a woman. It's a woman's business – it's not really a man's business. In my business I don't think women have any liabilities. But then in a business where men are the dominant sex, I think women would have a lot of liabilities . . . it's all according to the kind of business you're in. (aged 51, widowed, self-employed)

In sharp contrast to the innovators their most pertinent identities were those of 'mothers', 'wives', and 'women' rather than those defined according to business ownership. As two of them suggested:

I think men are men and women are women. Men should be boss – I've always felt that. I would hate to be equal . . . I like to think that a man is a man and not an extension of a woman. I like to think that a man is being treated like a man, as head of the house, that's all. My husband is always treated like that. It's a good thing. Marriages lasted longer years ago when men were treated like that . . . as far as I'm concerned, I don't want to be a boss. It's so much nicer to have a man to rely on, to lean on. It's much easier in life to have a strong man around. (aged 51, widowed, self-employed)

You have to have a very strong man [in an ideal husband–wife relationship]. I don't think it should be totally equal, psychologically. I think women respond better to strong men. I think when you have a weak man and a strong woman, she becomes a bitch – which is very unattractive – and he becomes a poor squashed mouse, which I find very unattractive . . . I don't like this terribly equal thing with men and women. I much prefer men to be very good at things – in fact, I rather demand that they have to be even better than I am at things. (aged 30, single, 7 employees)

Conventional businesswomen, then, do not see the need for restructuring of gender relationships and consequently they have little regard for a feminist movement which is collectively organized for the purposes of improving the social and economic position of women in general. They do not even view business start-up as a means for self-advancement and greater personal autonomy. Instead, it is generally seen as a source of income to supplement the earnings of husbands. If some innovators do recognize the importance of the women's movement, these owners are almost always derogatory in their remarks. They feel it serves no useful purpose – hardly surprising in view of their positive commitment to conventionally defined gender roles – and the following comments illustrate many of their attitudes.

Feminism? I don't like it. I think it's unnecessary. I was one of the first women to really start big business on my own and I certainly did not have any feeling that I wanted to do it for women. I wanted to do it for myself and my children. I w(l give them help if they needed it . . . But I certainly don't believe in the symbol of women burning their bras. I'm for all of us, not just for women. (aged 68, married, 950 employees)

Women's liberation! As I say, I look at it with rather wry amusement . . . some of it I dislike entirely – the student, shall we say, lesbian side . . . The side that says you mustn't use make-up, you mustn't do up your hair, you must wear those awful boiler suits. That's quite wrong. I also resent this phrase 'Only a housewife' – *they've* coined that phrase. I never heard that said when I got married . . . They've got the wrong end of the stick. They're bringing down something which shouldn't be brought down. I'm not a women's libber at all. (aged 60, widowed, 4 employees)

I think women's libbers are bloody stupid. I think any woman worth her salt ought to be proud. It's a fabulous thing being a woman. The women's libbers are their own worst enemy. They're impolite, they're aggressive, and they usually dress very badly. They lose that soft gentle touch that a woman should have. I don't want anything to do with them . . . I love being a woman because I have wonderful friends who do things for me and are kind to me . . . I wouldn't like to be changed at all. (aged 44, divorced, 3 employees)

I still think it's nice for women to have nice things and to concern themselves about make-up and to enjoy feminine things. I don't think that makes you less. I'm not going to burn my bra or anything like that . . . The extremists go too far, they really do. I don't care for the idea that I can't make a fuss over my man sometimes. I don't think that demeans me, if I want to make a fuss of him, cook him a super meal, wash something for him, or iron a shirt. I don't see that as a put-down . . . because he'll do things for me too – he'll sort out my hairdryer when it goes wrong. (aged 38, married, 1 employee)

The biggest disservice that has been done to women by women for what they thought was for women was women's lib . . . They have been aggressively non-female. I realize that you have to be perhaps extreme at times but a lot of damage has been caused . . . Ugliness in real-life business is a disadvantage. You can do things in a very attractive way and get away with it. I'm not saying that you should smile and be sexy and show your bosom. I *am* saying that by a pleasant attitude you can still be strong but firm. (aged 61, married, 3 employees)

This, then, concludes our discussion of conventional business owners. It seems to us that proprietorship has very few psychological or social effects for these women. For them, business ownership is seen to be entirely compatible with traditionally defined female identities and life-styles. It is, in other words, simply a means of making money in a manner compatible with their other domestic obligations, but avoiding the necessity of taking paid employment. Certainly, business start-up does not lead to a fundamental reappraisal of the general position of women in society. Perhaps this is important to note if only because, at present, it is likely that the greater majority of businesswomen are proprietors of this sort. Certainly, their attitudes and behaviour are in striking contrast to those radical business owners whom we discuss in the next chapter.

Notes: Chapter 6

1 Extensive evidence on women's orientations to paid work and the significance of financial influences, is provided in a recent survey commissioned jointly by the Department of Employment and Office of Population Censuses and Surveys (Martin and Roberts, 1984).

2 We recognize, however, that businesses which are not initially geared for growth can sometimes expand significantly almost against the will of the owner. This can alter the relationship between business and domestic obligations, as we outline in Chapter 9.

3 Once again, there are close parallels between the maternalist and paternalist employer strategies.

7

Creating Space: Radical Proprietors and Co-ownership

Despite a long tradition of co-operatives, co-ownerships and other forms of 'alternative' work organization within capitalist economies (Vanek, ed., 1975; Wright, 1979) the emergence of radical women's enterprises is relatively recent. In our terms, radical businesswomen are distinguished by their low commitment to entrepreneurial ideals and to conventional female roles. They usually see themselves as members of the feminist movement and their businesses as a means of improving the position of women in society (Goffee and Scase, 1983a). However, the link between business ownership and feminism is complex. For some, involvement in the women's movement encourages business start-up since this is regarded as a means whereby women can achieve, individually and collectively, a greater degree of self-determination. For others, by contrast, direct experience of male-imposed career blockages within conventional work organizations leads to the consideration of business ownership as an alternative. In this sense, there are similarities with the innovators, but while the latter compete with men according to male-defined 'rules of the game', the radicals regard their business ventures as part of a broader collective struggle to overcome, and eventually alter, these rules. Consequently, their businesses are not geared primarily to profit-making and any surplus which is generated is regarded as a resource which can be used to further the interests of women. The intention is to create a social and economic environment within which an alternative life-style can be pursued while, at the same time, providing services needed by other women. If successful, they 'create a space' which is largely free from men's influence both in and beyond the sphere of paid work. In this chapter we explore the distinctive strategies pursued by radical businesswomen, their motives for start-up and the implications of their enterprises for work experience, social relations and personal life-styles.

In this study we interviewed twelve women of this kind who were running nine businesses. These were engaged in a range of activities including printing, publishing, skills training, retailing and transport services. The enterprises took a variety of legal forms including, for example, limited liability companies, partnerships and co-operatives. All the women had founded or co-founded their businesses which, on average, had been established for five years. The most recent had been formed during the past year, while the longest had been trading for approximately ten years. Average annual turnover for these enterprises was £100,000, with three below £15,000 and the largest above £500,000. Of the nine enterprises, four had employees, with numbers varying from five to fifteen. Within the remaining five enterprises the number of 'partners' ranged from two to ten.

The average age of these proprietors was 34, the youngest being 26 and the oldest being 48. Only one of the twelve was married. Of the remainder, nine had never married and two were either divorced or separated. Three of them had children. The majority were university-educated and came from affluent middle-class backgrounds. Several were of overseas origin, with internationally mobile parents and considerable personal experience of geographical mobility. The social marginality often associated with such movement may well have encouraged their predisposition both to business ownership and the feminist movement (Goffee and Scase, 1983a).

As we have already noted, radical proprietors often share the innovators' experience of employment in large corporations where gender-related obstacles to career development had been encountered. Starting a business represents a strategy for overcoming such problems. But, in contrast to the innovators, radical women do not see themselves – nor wish to be seen by others – as 'entrepreneurs', indeed, they are determined to reject the motives, life-styles and attitudes typically associated with the conventional entrepreneur (Kets de Vries, 1977). Two of the women expressed this viewpoint as follows:

> I very much doubt whether women are going to get ahead by dint of being super businesswomen in the male mould . . . they end up supporting the status quo, which is what we are fighting . . . What

does the businesswoman of the year achieve by being business-woman of the year? She isn't going to get to be a man that way is she? And they're the ones who have power in this world. So she will be disappointed ultimately . . . When we originally got together we decided that the right thing to do in order to change the world was to take control of the processes of printing and publishing . . . Yet we are trying to publish books which we think will contribute to the creation of a kind of culture which we want to exist . . . We publish books because they are relevant to feminism . . . [And] a short definition of radical feminism is that what's wrong with the world and the reason women are oppressed is *men* – rather than, say, capitalism . . . men are the starting point, the primary affliction . . . What we're actually interested in is getting books out so that women will read them. We would like to be successful in business in order to provide money for that, in order to keep the presses going. But we would have gone off the point if we got too interested in business for the sake of business . . . It's *political* criteria which are the most important . . . So we print to eat and publish in order to change the world. (aged 26, single, 4 partners)

Mrs Thatcher's idea of economic independence and small business is based very much on capitalism. On the fact that you tread all over everybody else in the process. I don't think the women's movement can actually set up things like this business without having a strong sense of sisterhood – call it support, call it what you like. The only way we can do something like this is to have that sense of support, to support each other, bringing the whole mass of women up with us. Anything that we do that enables women to become more independent – for example, to be able to go out on their own because we provide a taxi service – this is what *we're* talking about. We're not talking about lining our own pockets which is what Margaret Thatcher wants people to do. (aged 34, single, 2 partners)

For these women, then, business start-up is neither geared to self-advancement nor to profit-making for its own sake; on the contrary, it is directed to collective feminist goals. The over-riding objective of business ownership is seen as the provision of various services for women which are not currently catered for elsewhere by, for example, the state, local authorities and private enterprises. The inadequacy of existing services is regarded as a reflection of the patriarchal organization and values of contemporary society. But, as three of the women explained, the existence of unsatisfied needs can provide an important basis for business start-up.

I set the business up. Basically I had this idea that a lot of women weren't particularly happy going about late at night in a cab with a man on their own. I became a mini-cab driver and I asked the women I drove around what they thought about the idea of starting a women's cab service. Without exception, they all said 'Great, when's it going to start?' . . . Basically, the reason it was set up was for the safety and comfort of women travelling about. A lot of women are very worried about violence from mini-cab drivers and violence from men in general so they don't want to walk the streets late at night . . . they just don't feel safe. Women who have been attacked prefer not to go in a car with a man alone, regardless of what he is like. Also, women with children often feel a lot happier being taken about by women drivers rather than men . . . So it's more than a taxi service, it's a support system for women. (aged 34, single, 2 partners)

Essentially this is a co-operative but the basic fundamental difference is that we're creating this business as a centre whereby we train women. They can get involved, get put on a skills and service register and train up other women. So you actually get skilled women training other women. Then we try and find them employment. We hope that women will phone in for services so that we actually keep the whole flow within the women's circle. It's the 'women help women' rationale, as opposed to setting up a business and breaking into an already established male market . . . It's non-profit-making . . . It's got mutually subsidizing facilities. One area subsidizes another, like the crèche, which we don't want to change. (aged 35, single, 10 partners)

We actually want the shop to be somewhere which is very accessible to women. We want to provide a range of literature and books that women want to read who aren't necessarily very strong feminists in any particular way. It means that a lot of the books we stock don't really have a political message of any kind but we consider them to be very well written by women who have a connection with the history of women's autonomy and women's expression. We do actually have a very strict stocking policy and we don't stock books which have nothing to do with the women's liberation movement.

So, for example, if Mrs Thatcher were to write her diaries we wouldn't stock it. We would get it for any woman who wanted it, of course. We didn't stock Mrs Wilson's diaries, and we haven't stocked Shirley Conran's *Superwoman*, to name a few that might ring a bell. And there are other popular sellers that we haven't been very keen on. (aged 29, single, 6 partners)

Support and service for women therefore takes overriding priority; profits which do accrue are usually 'ploughed back' and are regarded as the means by which feminist ends can be achieved. Indeed, many see their businesses as experiments in women's self-help which can be imitated by others in an effort to overcome their subordination.[1] There are few 'trade secrets', to the contrary business skills are regarded as a resource to be shared so that more women-owned enterprises can be established. As two of them said:

We're accountable to the women's movement. You can say that we've given the women's movement, or anybody who wants to try, an absolutely convincing model that it can be done . . . Publishing, books, writing, ideas, the lot. If you look at the map of England to work out what is happening in relation to women, you need never see a flat plain any more because there's a very strong model of how it can be done, which is incredibly valuable . . . It's de-ghettoizing. Nobody can say that it's a woman's enterprise and therefore it's going to be small. (aged 32, single, 8 employees)

The amount of support and good feeling that is created is incredible. Running a business gives women much more strength because it gives them the feeling of being in control of their own situation . . . I am helping women to become more autonomous . . . On Monday I am going to speak to a group of women in Cambridge who want to start up a women's taxi service . . . I've been in touch with the one that started in Hackney and said that if there are people in our area and we can't deal with them we'll pass them on to them and vice versa . . . So, there's no way that they're in competition. (aged 34, single, 2 partners)

If a major objective is to cater for the unmet needs of women, a further goal is to 'carve out' areas of feminist activity which are removed from male influences. Indeed, some proprietors, deliberately run their enterprises in a way which minimizes direct contact with men. This is achieved through explicitly providing goods and services for women only – for example, taxi services, printing facilities, training resources, and so on – and by giving priority to purchases from various female suppliers. In these cases, women-owned businesses are encouraged and an alternative 'feminist reality' is created within patriarchal capitalism. This provides a context within which it is possible to foster self-confidence, improve activities and advance feminist aspirations more generally. Three women expressed these views as follows:

We don't see ourselves as providing a service for men – we are providing a service for women. This is one of the areas where our own personal politics come out. We all feel very strongly that we do not want to put our energies into men at all. This comes out strongly in the way that we feel about men in the shop. We don't want them here . . . We want to save all our energies to help women . . . All of us have found that in working with men we simply don't have the space to express our feminist politics . . . We're an all-woman collective because we are working primarily for feminism. I've never come across any man who was prepared to do that, or, indeed, could do that. So, it's simply not operative to have men working here. Women have a deeper understanding of emotions and are prepared to put more energy and commitment into understanding each other's emotions. Therefore, we have a very different way of relating to each other personally . . . there's a spirit of generosity and of kindness and a lack of competition which you simply would not get anywhere else – even if it was a left-wing mixed alternative organiz-ation . . . Certainly, when men are working together, they work on the spirit and basis of competition which is an anathema to what we are doing here. We see ourselves as an expression of the women's liberation movement and competition is one of those things which oppresses women. (aged 29, single, 6 partners)

Printing goes back as a male profession a very long way in this country. The male printing world is quite well defined. Men expect, for instance, to work and to be paid overtime. It's crucial, in fact, to their incomes. But we don't provide that facility. If they're Fleet Street printers they expect to earn vast sums of money. They're not used to co-operatives . . . We're in a men's trade – a lunchtime drinking, hard, management-bashing world . . . When there were four of us it became a deliberate policy to exclude men because it was very useful. Women lack confidence because they're not expected to be in business or to run businesses and you're dealing with a male world of employees, bankers and everything. Women together give each other a lot of confidence and you have to make the decisions which normally, I suppose, we'd expect men to do. (aged 48, separated, 9 employees)

We wouldn't consider hiring men because we're a woman's firm. Our discussions with each other around women's issues are informed by our politics of the women's movement, and so on. Which is not to say that outside this place the women who work here do not have some engagement with men; they do. But here, in this place, issues and interests are for women. No, we wouldn't have men working here . . . We're not producing 'products', we're actually engaging with ideas . . . in terms of vocabulary and sensitivity to issues, it is in that way very different to deal with women than to deal with men. (aged 34, single, 5 employees)

These, then, are some of the major reasons for start-up. But where do radical women obtain finance? Conventional sources, such as the high-street banks are rarely considered on the assumption that the criteria of business viability which they apply would be inappropriate to this kind of enterprise. Instead, two other sources are used: their families and quasi-state institutions. Many of the women were from wealthy, middle-class backgrounds and they had taken advantage of this for obtaining funds. Indeed, they often justified these loans or gifts from wealthy relatives according to 'radical' ideals. One explained her use of inherited funds for business purposes in the following way:

I personally lent £5,000 to the shop to begin with. I inherited that money. It came from my grandfather's factory, the rotten old sod! And it just gave me personally enormous pleasure to put that into women, into a women's organization. (aged 29, single, 6 partners)

Alternatively, various types of subsidy or finance for business start-up may be obtained from quasi-state bodies such as the Manpower Services Commission, the Greater London Enterprise Board, the Co-operative Development Agency, different local council schemes, and various trusts and foundations. These appear to be specially important in London where several of the women in the study lived. Indeed, in view of the mutual distrust that often exists between radical businesswomen and male bankers, it is difficult to see how many of these enterprises could otherwise have started.

Even so, the financial aspects of business ownership frequently caused problems. Some argued the need to master skills of financial management in order to sustain their independence from men and foster an understanding of capitalist economics which many regard as a prerequisite in the struggle to overcome gender subordination. As the women argued:

> Women are held back by men who are in positions of power, mostly through money . . . Women are held back by a lack of self-confidence and our lack of ability to take big strides . . . We now have money and, politically, my understanding of male politics and of women's politics has developed into an understanding of how money works. And how men want money to work. And how they insist on it being such an important part of their transactions with each other. It's getting an insight into how capitalism works . . . Patriarchy includes capitalism – and other things besides. (aged 29, single, 6 partners)

> Men are so profit-orientated because a lot of the system, as it functions, is so success- and profit-orientated. That's the male ethos if you like. A lot of women are very suspicious of it and yet I feel that women can't actually have power until we have a certain amount of economic power. Until we have that we are bound all the time to come across men putting the kibosh on all we're trying to do. So, we've got to aim for economic viability. Some sort of economic independence – out of the system or in the system. Some say in how the economic system – which is basically the power base – is run. (aged 34, single, 2 partners)

However, the acquisition of financial 'understanding' within the context of a capitalist economy can itself cause considerable tensions within radical enterprises. Some women fear that feminist goals may be undermined by becoming too 'money orientated' and they feel uneasy about generating profits through trading with other women and by having women as employees. Radical women, therefore, experience a contradiction between the need to trade at a profit – or at least be self-financing – and their commitment to the egalitarian, non-exploitative aims of sisterhood. How do they cope with this? There seem to be two ways. First, they use any profits for the provision of additional services for women; and secondly, they take a similar rate of pay to their employees, if they have them. In these ways, the goals of business ownership and sisterhood are, to some extent, balanced. However, considerable tensions persist as the following accounts illustrate:

> There's a real kind of ethos about not making money out of the women's movement. Broadly speaking, I agree with that. If you're a political movement, the idea is to aim for radical change and not to make a living out of it . . . I've never restricted myself entirely to feminist staff . . . we offer our services to other co-ops, voluntary organizations, trade unions. It's still within the broad sphere of what we're concerned with. It's not the terrible compromise . . . I'm more interested in making the entire radical movement anti-sexist. I don't think I've sold the women's movement out. It's fairly obvious I'm not making a fortune . . . In fact, I do reject being totally poverty stricken . . . One of the reasons I felt quite funny about setting up business was that I thought quite a few people would be judgemental of me – and quite a few were – I must be one of the few people on the left of the women's movement who has actually run two businesses in her life. But the last thing in the world I see myself as is a businesswoman . . . The left generally has a very irrational attitude to money. (aged 32, single, 2 partners)

> This idea that feminists should be living in hovels – preferably a squat – and have virtually no money, or be on the dole and only do socially useful things for the good of their soul, and forget about living – you know, it's crazy! There's absolutely no reason why we should be on the breadline all the time. And if we create jobs for women we should be ensuring that we get a reasonable rate for our labour. (aged 34, single, 2 partners)

> The thing is that the shop has been doing very well. It's obviously arrived at the right time . . . so we haven't had any financial problems since we've opened and we have expanded. We're now twice the size that we were . . . The criticisms we've taken were not that we were more business than feminist; the criticisms were that we should not be in business at all! . . . [But] we do wish to pay

ourselves wages . . . we feel that one of the reasons the women's movement remains under the surface is that women have to give their work for nothing. We wanted very much to break with that tradition, to provide ourselves with a viable means of living! (aged 29, single, 6 partners)

As we discussed in Chapter 3, the concept of sisterhood is central to the women's movement and, accordingly, all the women we interviewed expressed a strong commitment to the ideal of co-operative work within small, non-hierarchical groups. Indeed, the development of these groups is often seen as a primary objective (Gould, 1979). Consequently, high priority is given to equally distributing work tasks, rotating jobs and sharing skills in order that the traditional divisions between 'managerial', 'clerical' and 'productive' activities are avoided. The characteristic emphasis upon flexible working relationships, personal expression and continual consultation about business operations and objectives is extensively illustrated in the remarks below.

Our organization derives very much from the development of feminist politics which arises from the consciousness-raising groups. Everybody has their right to speak and we work by consensus, which means that we talk about things until we all of us reach a decision that we're happy with. We don't take a vote. It means that nobody has more say than anybody else . . . We have a meeting once a week on Wednesday one hour before the shop opens – and it's usually a business meeting although personal things can come up . . . We've got this strong commitment to sharing all the jobs so that we all learn everything . . . there's bookkeeping, wage-paying, stock-keeping, ordering of books, helping out in the shop, knowing the stock – we do try and read as much of it as possible – cleaning the place, looking after the security and maintenance of the building . . . We have a more widespread filing system to make information available to everybody . . . We all take complete responsibility for what we're doing and we do *all* of the process. If you work in a straight bookshop you only take part in a particular part of the process. It's very seldom that you're actually given the power to order books. Whereas, anybody who works here has the power to do that from the first day they are here. (aged 29, single, 6 partners)

Everybody on the collective has the responsibility for reading and making comments – and for office work as well. We don't have secretaries. We do one day a fortnight each of office work . . . the satisfaction of working on something you're committed to is terribly important to me and working in a non-hierarchical way with other women is obviously just as important. The other advantages are the fact that there is no boss to insist on certain decisions being taken. Also, we are largely responsible to ourselves for the work that we do, the hours in which we work and the way we are in the office. In that sense I can't imagine that any of us will ever find a comparable working arrangement again . . . We have certain satisfactions which people in straight jobs cannot have because they have got to gear themselves towards a quite different intention . . . One of the advantages of working with an all-feminist collective is that support-ively you are encouraged to really develop how you feel about things in a way that is often stopped in business – even in all-women businesses. We actively encourage people to investigate themselves and develop themselves and to explore how they feel about things. (aged 38, divorced, 15 employees)

A basic thing when people come here is that they can do the job . . . [But] another criterion is that people should get on with the group. We have a three-month trial period for people coming in. They have to be compatible as we are actually very close as people . . . We have a meeting every day. We have lunch around that table every day so that in a certain sense one can bring *oneself* to work as opposed to bringing a façade to work. So you need to know that the people working together have certain levels of compatibility. I'm afraid I can't define them, they're feelings . . . [In other businesses] there'll be secretaries and bookkeepers and various servicing people – servic-ing the business. We don't have any of that superstructure. We don't have levels here at all – other than levels of expertise and length of time in the business – which are kind of natural. We don't have juniors . . . We usually get a majority decision . . . Usually it's resolved through discussion – we rarely go to a vote . . . We are individuals with needs and difficulties and problems. We have a very sympathetic attitude to mothers. We have a concept that we do things for mothers – It depends on the people here – what their needs are. As the need comes up, people will speak about it and then something will be decided. There's no fixed rule. (aged 38, single, 9 employees)

The commitment to sisterhood, then, is crucial for understand-ing how these businesses operate. It provides a set of principles for determining the organization of work and, often, the form of business ownership. But it is also the basis for two major dilemmas. First, the emphasis upon co-operation can limit business growth. This is because skills can be more easily shared within small tightly knit working groups than within larger enterprises where impersonality can undermine the ideals of sisterhood. Secondly, the need for continual consultation and personal expression can conflict with the necessity, within the context of a market economy, to make swift decisions on the basis of specialized expertise (Wajcman, 1983). These tensions between the administration of growing businesses and the ideals of feminism are well illustrated in the comments of four women.

At our full collective meetings, we have a meal in the evening at one of our houses. Again we talk about business, but it's also an opportunity to discuss more personal things. We have found increasingly that as our trade level is going up, we have less and less time to talk with each other during the day – and we miss this. This is one of the ways that working in a feminist collective comes to the surface. We want to find a very happy balance which includes the personal in our actual situation. We do have hiccups. When the shop first opened, we had a lot of time to talk about political issues and discuss things. In some ways, there's less need for that now because we know each other better, but this isn't the case for women who've joined the collective later. (aged 29, single, 6 partners)

It was a real shame that I started the business by myself because I became used to having to rely on myself to too great an extent. It would have been much better . . . if from the start there had been more women to work with . . . I'm very difficult to work with. I'm extremely tense about how everything turns out. I mind terribly. It's partly to do with the fact that I'm ultimately responsible for it all . . . It's quite hard for the people who work with me . . . I'm aware that it's very difficult for me to allow other people in the process of learning something to make a mistake. I rush in and save them from the mistake. Maybe it's better for someone to make a mistake and learn from it. But our mistakes are visible, so its really problematic . . . The problems are much more acute when you're trying to be groovy and political together and you deeply care about each other, yet, at the same time, you are the boss – you are ultimately responsible . . . It has to do with trying to work things out inside a situation which allows too little time for discussion and much too much work to be done all the time . . . Our business is to buy words and sell them to the public, so it's really naïve to imagine that we're not in that sense working as capitalists. But what we are trying to do is to modify it in terms of the way we work and the priorities we have. (aged 34, single, 5 employees)

We actually want to break into the commercial markets. It's very important for our credibility that we don't have that begging-bowl mentality. We want to be hard-headed businesswomen without the profiteering motive at the expense of other people's work . . . Although we're committed to collectivism, actually to be collective in every minor detail is an impossible way to run a business. So, collectivism, in its purest form, has to go to the wall. So there is an element of cynicism that could swell up. I don't see that as a problem as long as we make sure that people's positions aren't abused by retaining the trust and the sisterhood. Also, that we never exploit labour power and that we have specific areas of responsibility which we trust each other to actually fulfil. The hard-headedness and ruthlessness comes in if women don't live up to what's expected of them. Because it's just not one woman they're pulling down, it's the whole gender . . . We would need to eject people who didn't come up to scratch and not have nervous breakdowns about it. I just hope that that's not going to be a problem. (aged 35, single, 10 partners)

The decisions are so interrelated. If the magazine became much bigger, for example, it raises the question of how many people in a collective really can work effectively together. We would have to discover for ourselves what the optimum was . . . One of the problems here is that the work is so monumental and never-ending that maybe there is one area we neglect [already] . . . I feel we don't talk enough about our inner feelings in a collective situation. (aged 39, single, 15 employees)

In their attempts to avoid the more impersonal and economically calculative features of modern work organizations radical women clearly give priority to the cultivation of close personal relationships. If innovators often regard their businesses as substitutes for more emotional and intimate ties, the radicals deliberately create enterprises which will encourage the formation of such attachments. There is a strong expectation that participants will totally commit themselves to the collective enterprise which thus encompasses all facets of their personal life-styles. These businesses, then, are not simply alternative economic organizations, but also vehicles for the expression of feelings and emotions normally found within family and other intimate relationships. This fusion of work and non-work life is expressed in a physical dimension; within radical businesses, for example, discussion areas, crèche facilities, rest rooms, recreation spaces and other amenities normally associated with the conventional household are often provided. Such enterprises are, then, a 'way of life', as three of the women explained.

> We all work very hard, sometimes late in the evenings and at weekends. That's not only true of directors but of other people as well . . . We are individuals with needs and difficulties and problems . . . For instance, we had a pregnant woman and we actually paid her for nine months after she left here because she was married to a student, didn't have an income and didn't qualify for benefit . . . We bought a motorcar for somebody with a long journey and we've sent somebody to a health farm when they've been very overworked . . . The business has given the women a lot of support in terms of their private lives as well. We don't make that rigid distinction between work life and personal life – and that incorporates the lovers, the mothers, the fathers and all the problems. We bring them here, very very willingly. This is where we solve them. (aged 48, separated, 9 employees)

> Jill and Ann have a common interest in the Women Against Nuclear Power Group. Ann and I know each other well personally and Elaine and Jill knew each other very well. Susan and Lynn have a friendship of some years' standing . . . We don't go out and do things together because, in fact, we see so much of each other here . . . We have had a situation where two women in the collective were lovers for some time and that seemed quite all right. (aged 29, single, 6 partners)

> Actually, I must admit, that through the business I've made a lot of new friends because of the women I've helped, and women that have come to work in the office. A hell of a lot of really nice people . . . In terms of women working for themselves generally, I think the

amount of support and good feeling that is created is incredible. It gives women much more strength because it gives them the feeling of being in control of their own situation and that is absolutely vital. (aged 34, single, 2 partners)

In providing a 'total environment' for women these businesses sometimes serve as a refuge for those who have previously encountered severe personal unhappiness. In this sense, the feminist movement generally, and radical businesses in particular, can help women understand the external sources of personal depression and anxiety. One woman touched on this issue in the following terms:

> My personal life as a woman was very miserable until I understood that my unhappiness wasn't my personal problem but was something that women suffered because of what they are expected to do and the contradictory messages they are given . . . In some ways, it was as if my father treated me as a boy . . . I know the suffering I went through as I grew up and the misery of it. I would not only like to put a stop to that for myself, I would also like to produce a situation where that sort of thing simply doesn't have to carry on . . . If I hadn't discovered the women's movement at the time I did, I would almost definitely have been to see various psychiatrists and might have easily spent time in a mental institution. I was terribly, terribly depressed and completely unable to cope with my life. (aged 29, single, 6 partners)

It is not surprising that most of these women are personally opposed to marriage and the family. These are largely seen as a means whereby women are subordinated to men and children socialized into gender-prescribed roles. Many support the abolition of the family as a necessary step if women are to obtain a greater degree of self-determination. The comments of four of the women illustrate these views:

> I think marriage has very little to say for itself. Statistically speaking, women who get married suffer more mental distress than women who don't, and the converse is true for men. So we all know who marriage is for. I felt very early on that even if I had children, I wouldn't want to be married. It seemed to be a pointless exercise

. . . Even if I had children, it doesn't necessarily mean that I, as biological mother, would want to be the one who looks after them. Therefore, what on earth is marriage for? There just seems to be absolutely no point in it. It is specifically designed by the church and by the state to oppress women, to keep them isolated and, economically, to raise the next generation of workers free of charge. That's what it amounts to . . . We need to have much more sexual autonomy which means not having so many children – that's for starters. And it means us saying when *we* want children. (aged 29, single, 6 partners)

Marriage as an institution describes something totally different in a relationship than a man or woman who live together – or two women or two men who live together. Society looks on marriage in a certain way. Even if you don't look upon it in that way, it's impossible to live outside of what the institution says about you. It still says deeply conventional things about women, no matter how liberal the press or public attitude is. Behind it there is still the idea that it is women who must take primary responsibility for children, for the home and for caring for the man emotionally. (aged 26, married, 15 employees)

I'm not married and I don't think there'll ever be a need for me to be married . . . which is not to say that I wouldn't want to be in a relationship which involved a long-term commitment. But the institution of marriage wouldn't appeal to me at all . . . I wouldn't live in a conventional relationship. Nobody with a conventional view of life or of women would be with me! They wouldn't be attracted to me! I don't imagine that such a person need be a man anyway. It could even be a woman! My commitment is to women so it could be a woman! (aged 34, single, 5 employees)

These views on marriage are closely related to wider social perspectives. We have stressed throughout the manner in which radical businesswomen link their activities and attitudes to the feminist movement and gender-based subordination. This aware-ness has often been reinforced not only through occupational experience but also through geographical mobility. As socially marginal 'outsiders' some radical women are perhaps more likely to perceive the subtle influences which sustain female subordination than those who are firmly integrated within existing social networks and associated life-styles.[2] Such women, further, are more likely to start up businesses. As one of them explained:

> I do think that for English women it's incredibly difficult because they're not only socialized as women, there's also the whole class business of keeping people in a certain place – even if they're in a privileged class position. It means that they're very closeted by certain expectations laid upon their class . . . As an outsider, that's what I've observed. My feeling about English women is that very few of them are really expanding to their full potential . . . In fact, most of the women I know who are entrepreneurs are not English . . . they're foreigners here, which means that they're carving their own place. They haven't got family expectations breathing down their necks and they haven't got those class expectations. As an outsider, you're slightly above and beyond those particular kinds of restrictions. (aged 34, single, 5 employees)

Despite their own efforts – and in marked contrast to other businesswomen – most radical owners expressed a strong feeling that the economic and social circumstances of women in the 1980s were deteriorating. Recession and government policies were said to be increasing unemployment, reducing career prospects and forcing women back into the domestic sphere to perform their traditional roles. If there had been any improvements in the position of women during the postwar era these were now seen to be seriously threatened. Three women expressed these pessimistic views in the following way:

> I think the future looks terrible. The fact that there's such an economic recession is going to mean that everyone who is vulnerable – and women are very vulnerable indeed – is going to get worse off. Very bad news. You just have to look at the way the press deals with feminism now. There's most definitely a backlash. During the 1970s when economically things were easier, there was much more leniency towards things that were seen as somewhat different. But now it's all backs to the wall and right is might and all that sort of crap. (aged 34, single, 5 employees)

> Until the whole system changes, women are going to be in the same position or a worsening situation. Women are in a worsening position now, there is no doubt about that whatsoever. When

there's unemployment, women are the first to be unemployed, and women's wages go down. Nursery schools are closing, as are crèches . . . the whole position of women is getting worse . . . As long as this system lasts, it will continue to get worse. I don't think this is a bend in the recession – I think this recession is the end of the system, or the beginning of the end . . . I see structural change as inevitable. (aged 48, separated, 9 employees)

At the moment, the gains that women have made are either at a slight standstill or even moving backwards. It's not just Thatcher's government. It's a time of economic recession and it's also a time of ideological reaction . . . It's just a question of one step forward and two steps back. I would see feminism as getting stronger and stronger but not necessarily the women's movement. (aged 39, single, 15 employees)

What should be done? For most, the major task for the women's movement is to restructure society since only in this way can gender relations be fundamentally altered. Socialism – with the production of goods and services for need rather than profit – is seen by most to offer the long-term solution.[3] Present-day capitalism, by contrast, with its inherent dependence upon exploitation and competition, is regarded as incapable of bringing about the real liberation of women. Within the short term, many argue the need for positive discrimination so that, for example, women who want to start their own businesses should be given special state-funded assistance. These opinions contrast sharply with those of the innovators who, although in favour of equal-rights legislation and against sex discrimination, are opposed to women obtaining 'special treatment'. In their view, government assistance should be directed to *all* small businesses and not to female-owned enterprises in particular. The contrasting views of radical women are expressed in the following:

I would like to say one thing: I think until women are a lot more equal to men, I would like to see not just non-discrimination towards women, but *positive* discrimination for women in areas such as jobs, housing and education. I would actually like to see some positive discrimination for women as opposed to laws which say you can't discriminate between men and women. Women have got to the stage where it is perfectly possible for them to do so much more. It's not going to be possible unless they are positively discriminated for. (aged 34, single, 2 partners)

It will be really good to have women business owners helped specifically. Given that there's money around, precious little of it gets into the hands of women – that's my feeling. There's also very specific pressures on women's businesses. There are a lot of people who would like women's businesses not to succeed because we *are* challenging the status quo, which is that everything should be run by men . . . If we make a small mistake, very much is made of it, whereas if the mistake is by Joe Schmloe Ltd, then nobody would even notice it. We have to be *extremely* successful to be as successful. (aged 34, single, 5 employees)

The views expressed by radical businesswomen indicate little commitment to profit-making, business growth, or the pursuit of personal careers for their own sake. Instead, the major driving force of these enterprises is the provision of various need-related services as defined by the priorities of the wider women's movement. Both the innovators and the radicals reject conventional female roles but they differ in the ways in which they attempt to overcome subordination; whereas the former try to 'beat men at their own game' and, therefore, fully integrate themselves within patriarchal institutions, the latter try to carve out spheres of feminist autonomy. But how do they differ from the domestic traders who, similarly, are not committed to profit-making? This is discussed in the next chapter.

Notes: Chapter 7

1　In this sense, they looked upon their enterprises as 'business models' for other prospective proprietors in the same way as individual women are sometimes regarded as 'role models' (see Chapter 3).

2　Further evidence on the mobility and marginality of women who achieve is provided in Epstein and Coser (1980).

3　It must be emphasized that the socialism envisaged by the women we interviewed fundamentally transforms patriarchal capitalism; in this sense, it is normally regarded as distinct from the socialism currently practised in Eastern European States.

8

Business as Pleasure: Domestic Traders

Domestic traders, in a similar manner as the radical women we interviewed, are not committed to profit-making. For them, business start-up is geared to achieving a number of personal goals which, for one reason or another, cannot be attained through paid employment. Often they are unable to pursue careers because of their domestic commitments and because of factors which limit their geographical mobility. Consequently, business ownership is seen to offer opportunities for the exercise of particular skills and talents, and a means for self-fulfilment within constraints stipulated by domestic relationships (Goffee and Scase, 1983a). Such women tend to be middle-class and to be married to managerial and professional employees with the effect that economic compulsion is rarely the prime motive for start-up as it was for many of the conventional women that we interviewed. Instead, and, in addition to the search for self-fulfilment, proprietorship is usually regarded as a means for obtaining a certain degree of personal autonomy. Thus, it enables them, if only for limited spheres of their lives, to discard their roles as mothers and wives and to take on independent identities associated with their businesses. How then, do they run these businesses and with what effects for their attitudes and behaviour?

In our study there were thirteen women who may be regarded as illustrative of this pattern of business ownership. Their trading activities included dressmaking, pottery, interior furnishing, floral arrangement and engraving. All had started their own businesses which, on average, had been in existence for seven years; the longest having been established for twenty-four years and the most recent, for less than twelve months. Annual turnover ranged from £1,000 to £25,000, with the average being £7,000. Ten of the thirteen proprietors had no employees, while the remainder regularly used part-time workers.

The ages of our group of domestic traders ranged from 30 to 54 years with the average being 39 years. Twelve were married, one was divorced and all bar one had children. It is only by reference to the nature of these family relationships that it is possible to understand the start-up and functioning of their businesses. Almost all of the women were married to managerial and professional employees and by comparison with the conventional proprietors they were highly educated and well-qualified. Many of them had been employed previously in various middle-range clerical, administrative and managerial jobs in large-scale organizations. On getting married, or shortly afterwards, they had given up their careers to have children. They had then started their own businesses when the children demanded less of their time but always in ways that were compatible with family relationships. As such, their experiences are in sharp contrast with the innovators who give total priority to business success and neglect personal relations, and with conventional proprietors who generally start their businesses for economic reasons. For these women, the motives are almost entirely associated with self-fulfilment, the exercise of creative skills and the search for personal autonomy. But, again, these need to be interpreted within the context of husband–wife relations in the middle-class family (Pahl and Pahl, 1972; Edgell, 1980; Cooper, 1982). Often the husband is upwardly mobile by virtue of enjoying a varying degree of success within his career. At the same time, this leads to work becoming a central life interest such that family and other personal relationships can often become secondary and even be neglected. Accordingly, their wives can feel isolated and estranged from the men into whose success they have directly and indirectly contributed. They can be further dissatisfied if only because family responsibilities have forced them to give up their own careers and to under-utilize their own creative skills. Business start-up for such women, therefore, offers opportunities for coping with these dilemmas. Indeed, it is often the only route available to them because of the absence of suitable jobs and career opportunities within particular geographical localities. Whereas it is assumed as normal for wives to move homes because of their husband's jobs, the reverse is very rarely the case (Rapoport and Rapoport, 1976). All these factors, then, shape the pattern of business start-up among these women. The following comments illustrate some of these and particularly the importance of the need for self-fulfilment and personal autonomy.

I didn't want a 9 to 5 job. I wanted to do something in my own time
. . . one of the reasons why I chose to be self-employed was because I
enjoyed being at home more than being in an office or anywhere else
. . . I think that when my son went away to boarding school that if I
hadn't done something it would have harmed my marriage . . . As a
housewife you can get taken for granted too quickly and you become
too reliable. Being a housewife is sometimes not thought to be
something praiseworthy . . . I'm much happier that I've got my
own life and my husband has his life. He is supportive of the
business but not part of it . . . I can parcel out my time as is needed
and certainly the most important things in my life are my husband
and son. Therefore, during the school holidays I spend far more time
mending my son's toys than I do mending china. I don't let the
business encroach. (aged 37, married, self-employed)

I was asked to do it originally for a charity bazaar and then the
following year I decided to do it for myself because I rather enjoyed
doing it . . . and partly because my husband was away a great deal,
my sons were away at boarding school and I needed something to
keep myself occupied . . . It also fits in with the garden and the fact
that I want to travel with my husband on business . . . As a person I
always have to have a project in front of me. I have to have
something that I must do. Without that I might not be a very
pleasant person to live with . . . But I look at my business as coming
third. Both my husband and son are much more important to me
that doing the dried flowers. Although it seems at times that they
impinge, they don't in fact. I would always drop the business for
either . . . Even if I was doing some other kind of business it would
be the same. I would always make the family number one. (aged 38,
married, self-employed)

The business basically meets a need for me to find a medium to
express myself as a person – an individual . . . My husband always
encouraged me. He realized the benefit to me, of making me into
much more of a whole person . . . The business has been a great
asset. It's given me a sense of my own value. And given *them* (my
husband and children) a sense of my value, which I think is very
important. So we're not dependent in a subversive way upon each
other . . . Of course, the children are away from home now and my

husband is often away all the day up in London, and in the evenings as well. So I really now run my life fairly independently. But when the family are at home certainly that's when I make sure I am free for them. (aged 54, married, self-employed)

My skills are a gift – they allow me to do a job which I can do at home. There are very few jobs that let you do that . . . In some ways my ideal would be to see my husband off in the morning and take my children to school. That is my ideal. Then I would settle down to do a day of gentle housework. But I don't know, I always think that I have to work . . . I think it is a necessity to feel that you are still worthwhile. That you are not just a drudge . . . Overall, I'm very lucky to have a job in which I can incorporate a home and children. This is the epitome of what I wanted. I've got it and I'm very lucky. (aged 34, married, self-employed)

Domestic traders, then, do not make a choice between their businesses and their families. On the contrary, they give priority to the needs of their husbands and children and it is within these parameters that they start trading. Indeed, many of these ventures are only viable because of the financial back-up of their husband's earnings. Further, since most of these businesses are run from homes various overheads such as heating, lighting and telephone can be used for both domestic and business purposes and accounted for in the most efficient manner for taxation purposes.

Because the life-styles of middle-class wives are so heavily shaped by the occupational demands of their husbands, it has been claimed that they become incorporated within their husband's jobs (Finch, 1983). This incorporation is considered to consist of two dimensions. First, the husbands' occupations determine the parameters within which wives' living standards and life-styles are structured and, secondly, the women contribute to their husbands' jobs through providing a range of material and psychological supports. Clearly, some jobs will lead to a greater degree of incorporation than others. Some husbands, for example, have occupations which require only a limited input by their wives because such jobs are not particularly psychologically demanding and because it is possible for there to be a sharp distinction between work and non-work life-styles. Many lower-grade, white-collar and routine manual occupations are of this sort. On the other hand, there are those jobs which are very demanding in both time and psychological energy and which tend to impinge upon all aspects of employees' life-styles. Thus, work has to be taken home in the evenings and at weekends, clients and colleagues are expected to be entertained and certain leisure activities and interests are assumed by the corporation. Many middle-class occupations have these demands and it is expected that wives become fully involved, if only indirectly, with their husbands' jobs and they, themselves, acquire identities which are vicarious; that is, identities which are derived from, and dependent upon, those of their husbands.

Domestic traders start their own businesses for reasons of self-fulfilment and for developing their own identities but this is always within general parameters stipulated by their husbands' occupations and careers. This, in turn, has important implications for their businesses since it acts as an impediment to growth for at least two reasons. First, such women are reluctant to acquire earnings which are greater than those of their husbands because this would challenge assumptions which middle-class wives have about the priority of their husbands' careers. Secondly, and more importantly, business growth would create demands on their time and life-styles which would threaten the pattern of family and conjugal relationships. These points are illustrated in the following:

Jealousy can be a difficult thing. I've always been successful in my work. It's worked well at home . . . There was a time when I was doing much better than my husband financially and it caused the most dreadful rift. It caused us to split up, to live apart for six months. When we eventually got back together again, I realized that he had to be the top dog – whether he was or not didn't matter. He had to feel that he was still needed. I'm a very independent person and sometimes I really had to make myself say to him, 'Can you help me please, I can't cope'. (aged 34, married, self-employed)

I have a battle keeping it small and keeping it within the family because I know I could actually make it quite a big business and that would destroy the marriage part of it. It's a very fine line you walk along there . . . You suddenly know you could be out there doing as much as the man in your life. And the man in your life doesn't like that, however much he might say otherwise . . . I've got to think hard of my husband because it definitely affects him if I'm earning more. He loves me earning, he loves me working, but he doesn't like to feel that I could actually look after myself. I can see that being quite a problem. They do like you to be dependent upon them. (aged 36, married, 3 employees)

Although business start-up is rarely motivated by financial considerations and there is very little commitment to growth, it does not mean that economic factors are entirely absent. Such businesses can be important sources of supplementary earnings which enable various privileges and benefits to be purchased for their families, some of the more important of these, for example, include private education, second cars, holidays abroad and weekend cottages. The following comments illustrate this:

I started up because I wanted to educate the children. Rightly or wrongly, that was the sole reason for doing it. It was only because I felt the boys needed to be given a good education. Even now, I, myself, get very little out of the business because the school fees are enormous. It's all for the children . . . I'm supported wholly by my husband because I'm using the money to educate the children . . . and because of that, the children have got a far happier mum than they would have had. (aged 37, married, 1 employee)

I remember saying when we first started that if I could earn £6,000 a year from the business to pay my son's school fees that would be fine. That was my original intention, just to bring in enough money so that the children could be educated privately. (aged 40, married, 4 employees)

When I first went into business . . . I was faced with the prospect of paying the children's school fees. I really felt ill equipped to do this . . . but eventually I established the business. It's been terribly hard work . . . If I hadn't felt that I had to pay the school fees, I would have given up. (aged 40, remarried, self-employed)

If, however, there are such economic motives for business start-up, these are normally subordinated to the quest for personal autonomy and self-fulfilment. This, in turn, often leads to the setting up of businesses geared to the low-volume production of high-quality goods and services. Further, since these women have very limited marketing skills they hedge their risks by developing 'books' of regular customers with whom they trade on a long-term basis. Consequently, there is no need for them to spend money in advertising and the relationship between trader and customer becomes close and personal. Their businesses, therefore, provide opportunities for the formation of the extensive social networks within which business is conducted (Scase and Goffee, 1981). As a result, profit-making is constrained by various non-economic criteria and by personal obligations. These points are illustrated in the following:

I felt the need to do something on my own . . . I wanted to express my own self . . . What gives me greatest satisfaction is creating something from a lump of clay which is a living thing. I know it sounds funny but it is, clay is alive. Being able to produce something, that's absolutely marvellous, that's the thing. As soon as I've made something, I don't want to know about it. I've got to sell it, but really my brain is immediately thinking of the next piece. (aged 52, married, self-employed)

Customers come and say, 'I don't know what you'll be able to do with me. I've been to other places and nobody has been able to make me look good.' That's it – it's the challenge. It's making people feel that they like themselves instead of feeling as if there's no hope . . . I do it as a personal satisfaction. I've wanted to do this since I was 9. It was almost like a gift from God really. It's just something that I feel is a gift and I want to be able to use it. (aged 34, married, self-employed)

I just love doing it for myself, because I feel good. That's why I started. I need to do the exercise so it makes me feel good. When the customers come in and say that they really feel much better, it's fantastic. You get a lot of feedback from the classes . . . And the reason why I'm so successful is because I'm totally relaxed about the whole thing. If I got up in the mornings knowing that I had to feed my family and pay the rent and do this whether I liked it or not, I would have a whole different attitude to it . . . The customers know I love it and they can sense it . . . Once I start, to me, it's like being on stage and by the time I've finished I feel fantastic. (aged 36, married, 3 employees)

I'm not a very money-orientated person. Money doesn't mean a lot to me. Money for money's sake, I don't see that . . . For me, the most satisfying thing is just to have done a good job at the end of the day. That's really all. My father always worked for himself and I think it's how you're brought up – to do a good day's work for a good day's pay. (aged 37, married, 1 employee)

I get most satisfaction from delivering and having customers say they like the flowers. Or, having just finished an arrangement – I would say I get a great deal of pleasure from that . . . I get least satisfaction from the production line aspect of it – when people ask you to produce four or five of the same thing again. (aged 38, married, self-employed)

These women, then, want to be self-fulfilled through the exercise of their various talents and craft skills. Consequently, they restrict their trading to a low level even when their goods and services are in high demand, because only in this way can they produce them at a sufficiently high quality for their regular customers. They are normally very reluctant to expand their volume of trading since this would require a more 'rational' or 'business-like' approach which would destroy key sources of job satisfaction and, at the same time, undermine the personal relationships which they develop with their customers. This, in turn, could threaten the 'secure' bases of their businesses and expose them to greater risks in the market. These attitudes are captured in the following:

I see myself more as a craftswoman than an entrepreneur. I'm not going out to sell what I can do because, basically, I've always done it for friends and friends of friends. I've never had to advertise, ever. I have always had enough business coming in not to have to go and find it. (aged 42, married, self-employed)

It's always been my idea that we would be a little bit expensive but that we would give a very good personal service – turn the orders round quickly, be nice to deal with, helpful, and so on. I think it pays off in the long run. A good core of our customers, even though they know they can get it cheaper somewhere else, will always come back to us because they know they wouldn't have to wait. There will be no muddles. (aged 40, married, 4 employees)

My customers initially were neighbours, then somebody tells somebody else. It's amazing how it snowballs . . . I'm not really competing with anybody. Three months is nothing for a customer to wait.
It's such an individual thing, they'll wait for you . . . It's a very
specialist thing and obviously somewhat expensive . . . I survive
because I give service. I bend over backwards for people and run
around after them. I do things you wouldn't get in a shop. Somewhere along the line I suppose you've got to stick your neck out and
get bigger but I can't see me doing that . . . I was doing a bit more
business a couple of years ago but I thought 'What's it all about? I'm
working very hard and raking in money and life is slipping by.' I
like to keep it manageable and personal. You can have a lot of people
working for you but your worries are increased and you lose contact.
Is it worth it? (aged 37, married, 1 employee)

Although these businesses are firmly structured within family
relationships, they have little direct impact upon husband–wife
relationships. Conjugal roles are rarely reorganized with husbands
undertaking a greater share of the domestic tasks so that their
wives can devote more time to their businesses. This is partly
because both husbands and wives regard these businesses as secondary to the demands of their husbands' careers and to other family
obligations. If these men do have any involvement it is largely in
terms of back-up rather than through a regular, long-term
commitment. This, of course, is in sharp contrast to the experiences of women who are married to business owners (Scase and
Goffee, 1980b, 1982; Goffee and Scase, 1982b). In these, women
are often forced to jeopardize their own career prospects and even
give up their full-time jobs in order to help in their husbands'
businesses. Without this generally unpaid assistance many male-
owned businesses would not get off the ground. Further, all
household tasks are undertaken by their wives, enabling them to
devote the whole of their energies to their businesses. By contrast,
these women traders not only run their own businesses almost
single-handedly, but also retain responsibility for the domestic
sphere. If husbands do help in their businesses it is only in a very
limited manner and usually restricted to financial matters. As
managerial and professional employees these men normally possess
the necessary skills for dealing with bank managers, tax inspectors,
accountants, solicitors, and others. They often feel compelled to

undertake these tasks because their wives do not possess the necessary business or financial skills. Consequently, many of them become dependent upon their husbands for the purpose of being independent traders. If in the exercise of their creative skills they can enjoy a degree of personal autonomy and self-fulfilment this is often constrained by their husbands' willingness to act as financial negotiators and bookkeepers. The following statements illustrate the supportive but essential role of many husbands:

Quite frankly, without my husband I wouldn't have got as far as I have because, bless him, he's always in the background supporting me. He's the back-up. He leaves me to do the creative work – the firing and the glazing and all the actual pottery – but if things break down or things go wrong, he's there as the prop. We are a family unit here . . . To be honest, I haven't found obtaining credit too difficult   because I have my husband behind me. But standing on my own, there would be no way. (aged 52, married, self-employed)

My husband is interested in the business from a distance. I don't think he'd particularly like to get directly involved with any of it. He'd rather I sorted out everything . . . [But] he is supportive in a way. For instance, he told me the right firm to go to, to get the letter-headed paper – one that he found cheap and reliable. It's that sort of thing, but it's definitely from a distance. He doesn't really want to get involved. (aged 30, married, self-employed)

My husband is very good actually. He, too, would very much have liked a business of his own. But my business is the nearest he's got. There have been some times in the past when things have been dodgy and I've felt like chucking it all in and he's kept me going . . . He also chases up debts and he delivers things for me and makes awkward phone calls which I haven't got the courage to make. I like him to be stronger than I am . . . Then, when I go and see the bank manager, I'm just an appendage to my husband . . . When I wanted some money to buy a van, the bank manager said 'Bring your husband down' . . . My husband previously banked elsewhere and it was put very nicely that he would have to transfer his account. He did. He's very good like that. (aged 37, married, 1 employee)

I am as I am because I am supported by my husband . . . I think that certainly the biggest strength is the support of my husband and family, and not having to look over my shoulder all the time wondering where the next penny is coming from. That, obviously, has to play a major part for the business. (aged 54, married, self-employed)

Such support by their husbands, however, is never allowed to interfere with their careers. Life-styles are shaped by the pervading influences of their husbands' jobs rather than by their own businesses and the needs of the former always override those of the latter. As four of them explained:

> The ideal relationship means trying to work when your husband works and always being there when he needs you. And if he's suddenly got to have a business dinner party, not to say, 'Oh, I'm sorry, I'm working' . . . My husband might take that once or twice but if it was six times in a row, he'd be cheesed off . . . In general, we socialize much more with my husband's friends than with my friends. I think this is something that a wife often falls into. I mean, a wife will often take all the business dinners but a husband will not do the reverse. They just won't do it. (aged 36, married, 3 employees)

> My husband runs his own business as an adviser in investments . . . Each year I have six weeks when I go off with him on business, when I share in his job and meet the people he does business with. So now we have very close friends right across the United States because we don't differentiate between business and real friends . . . [But] our friends are very much *his* business friends . . . I suppose my work has, to a certain extent, given me friends of my own but I don't really have a lot of time for them. (aged 54, married, self-employed)

> I do have my own friends . . . but I have two sorts of life really. I have to do a lot of socializing with the sort of life that my husband is involved in. So I'm very much involved in socializing with his colleagues and also, with visiting the theatre, because he writes theatre books as well. (aged 40, remarried, self-employed)

> I don't expect my husband to be bound up in my interests. We can both contribute to each other. It's extremely interesting listening to his day-by-day news of how his business is going. But he doesn't take any interest in my dressmaking and I don't expect him to. It's because he has got a much more fun business. (aged 42, married, self-employed)

All of this means that many of these domestic traders have three sets of functions to perform. First, they provide a range of direct and indirect social and emotional supports that are crucial for their husbands in their pursuits of careers. Secondly, they are almost single-handedly responsible for the organization of the domestic sphere. Thirdly, they are running their own businesses, and it is only this which enables them to enjoy a degree of personal independence. If, however, their husbands become redundant or opt out of their careers the nature of their businesses can fundamentally change.[1] In such circumstances their husbands may become more directly involved and the enterprise can be restructured on a more 'efficient' basis and geared to growth. Accordingly, these businesses may cease to operate as outlets for self-fulfilment but instead, become oriented to profit maximization. As two of them explained:

My husband and I have reached an important point in our lives where we are going through a tremendous change. We've had to rethink a lot of things . . . [because] my husband has just had to sell off part of his business. We've been forced into these circumstances, unfortunately . . . Over the last two years I've had to assist a great deal in his business but now that could swing right round and he may have to help me much more in mine . . . I've been running this set-up for some sixteen years . . . [but] I suppose, in a way, I'm now thinking of expanding it – of more diversification . . . [so] commercial success is important. The decision to do my own thing must also encompass the fact that it's got to be profitable. (aged 52, married, self-employed)

My husband left his job and joined the business about two years ago . . . His company had just brought him back to England and he found he'd been abroad too long – about twelve years altogether. No one knew him in the company here and it really was better that he left. He had always wanted to work for himself anyway . . . It just happened that he was dissatisfied and I was getting into deep water running the business entirely on my own. So this is why he joined . . . We work pretty well together . . . He's much better at some things than me. I'm inclined to keep things fairly close to my chest, but he is different. He thinks, for example, the bank should be told everything, so he prepares monthly profit and loss accounts and balance sheets. Actually, this has paid off and now we don't seem to have any problem. (aged 40, married, 4 employees)

But how does business ownership affect the identities of these women? It seems to have only very limited effects – except for the psychologically 'liberating' experience of a greater degree of personal autonomy – if only because most of their trading is conducted with other women in the retail or personal services sectors of the economy. Further, they avoid the threatening attitudes of many bank managers, solicitors, and so on by using their husbands as negotiators and as their representatives. Thus, their identities as predominantly 'middle-class wives' are not challenged by their business proprietorship. The advantage of trading with other women was emphasized by one of the traders we interviewed.

> I haven't had special difficulties because what I'm doing is such a woman's thing, you see. I haven't got up against any men in this . . . I mean, women prefer to be taught by a woman. I haven't had any battles with men. My business is for women . . . it's a very feminine business. It would probably be different if I was working in an office and I was trying to get up there with the guys. I would probably find it much tougher. I would probably have a different attitude. But I can allow myself to be feminine in what I am doing. And if you are in hairdressing or clothes you can be feminine. As for me, I would never want to be in direct competition with a man. (aged 36, married, 3 employees)

Consequently, many of these proprietors expressed rather 'traditional' attitudes about the position of women in society and, in many ways, these were rather similar to those of the conventional proprietors we interviewed. For instance, they stressed the nature of the biological differences that exist between men and women and assumed that these have direct consequences for their respective roles in society. Generally, they subscribe to the desirability of traditional gender roles which they regard as just and complementary. As such their experience as traders does not lead them to challenge these assumptions, as the following comments illustrate.

> I think there's a great deal to be said for the view that women's main responsibilities are as housewives and mothers. I think we've gone too far from the solid home base . . . I think it's a myth that most women want to be something they are not . . . I think men are men

and women are women. It's ridiculous to think that they can be absolutely equal . . . women can do things perfectly well without anyone having to say that they need to be equal to men or the same as men. I don't think there can be equality of opportunity because we're different from the start . . . How can you have equality of opportunity if children's reactions to things are different? It happens with animals too – female dogs or cats react differently. It's just nonsense to say there is no difference. And if there is a difference you cannot have equality of opportunity. (aged 38, married, self-employed)

I think it's terribly important that the role of women as housewives and mothers doesn't die out . . . The mother is instrumental in giving a child its childhood and a child should not suffer on that score for the sake of pin money for the home . . . I think there are basic differences – men and women will never think alike and they shouldn't try to make themselves equal. Women can go a long way just because they are women. (aged 37, married, self-employed)

Attitudes have been handed down from grandmothers and through mothers . . . the view that women should be at home looking after the children . . . [But] there are an awful lot of women who are content with that and they don't want any more. Society seems to be pressuring them to feel they're no good if they stay at home and cook the dinner – they feel they ought to be doing something more. That's giving women a lot more trouble than anything else. Why don't they leave them alone? . . . I don't see that we should be any different from how we are at the moment . . . I don't actually want pure equality with men. I still like a man opening a door for me and walking on the roadside of the pavement and those little niceties. (aged 30, married, self-employed)

From these comments, it follows that many of these traders do not think that women who start their own businesses should receive any special treatment from government, banks and other financial institutions. In any case, they argue, most women are married and supported by husbands.[2] If, then, there is to be special provisions for small business owners, these should be directed to men since as husbands and fathers, they have 'extra responsibilities'. One of them made the following comment:

Why should there be special help for women? Why not for men as well who are starting businesses? They need help just as much –

probably more so because they have wives and families to support. And it must be very difficult for a man to suddenly branch out on his own. They work for someone for years, see that they are getting no personal satisfaction out of it and then they branch out. They are gambling absolutely everything. They are giving up full-time regular employment with money at the end of every month. Whereas usually when a women starts her own business she has someone to support her. (aged 36, divorced, self-employed)

In view of these attitudes, it is hardly surprising that many of these women were hostile to the women's movement. They often feel that it does not recognize that many women prefer to be full-time housewives and mothers. Indeed, some argued that feminism, by directly attacking the family, was undermining society and the conventional nurturing role of women which they valued highly. Thus, unlike the innovators or the radicals, their businesses neither stem from, nor lead to, a conscious questioning of sex discrimination or gender subordination. Put simply, these women are satisfied the way things are and oppose the changes sought by the women's movement. The following remarks are illustrative.

It's important that the man always feels stronger. I really do feel that. I don't agree with women's lib at all. I think that we can get much more done using the feminine wiles that we have been given . . . I think the feminists are really messing up a lot of peoples' lives. I don't agree with it. I feel that we would get a lot more done if we were *more* feminine. (aged 36, married, 3 employees)

I don't see a need for any change . . . I'm not a women's libber. I'm quite happy the way I am. I haven't thought about it, to be quite honest. It doesn't interest me at all . . . I don't think a woman is quite so strong as a man. I know I'm not. I don't think I'd be able to make a decision, comparing myself with my husband. You know, I'm too soft for that. (aged 37, married, self-employed)

I think we had far more equality years ago before all those women libbers started messing things about. We just knew how to handle it and keep it quiet. Now it has been brought out in the open we've lost a lot of advantages. I enjoy men standing up for me and opening doors when I walk into a room. It's all part of being a woman. But now women have fought for equality, we're not getting these little things which mean such a lot. (aged 36, divorced, self-employed)

I know some women who are terribly happy as 'just' housewives and mothers. They find enormous creativity and satisfaction . . . I think too much has been said about sex and equality. It doesn't interest me. I don't have any time at all for the women's movement. They're all rather masculine and male-orientated and, really, they are going against their natures. (aged 54, married, self-employed)

It seems, then, that proprietorship has only limited effects upon the personal identities, attitudes and behaviour of these women. Generally, they regard their businesses as means for self-expression within the parameters of existing gender roles and family relationships. As with conventional businesswomen, there are few consequences for personal life-style even though motives for start-up differ. However, the contrast with the radicals and innovators, whose business activities question gender identities and relations, is far stronger. We turn our attention to these differences in the final chapter and assess the extent to which the various types of business ownership discussed in this book allow women to achieve a greater degree of self-determination.

Notes: Chapter 8

1 In the 1980s and 1990s the incidence of executive redundancy and other forms of career break are likely to increase (Handy, 1984). We return to this theme in Chapter 9.
2 In Britain, less than two-thirds of all women are married and divorce rates are increasing (Reid, 1982).

9

Conclusions: the Prospects for Female Proprietorship

Our aim in this book has been to describe the experiences of women who start their own businesses. In particular, we have tried to determine the extent to which business proprietorship enables them to overcome various forms of gender-based subordination. As a framework for discussion we have differentiated them according to their attitudes towards profit-making and the extent to which they are prepared to accept or reject conventionally defined female roles. The four types we identified are inevitably tentative and must be regarded as simplifications, if only because few individuals fit neatly into any one of the four categories. Further, there are wide differences in the experiences of women who start their own businesses which are largely accounted for by factors other than those of attitudes towards profit-making and the acceptance of conventional female roles. Finally, our typology is a simplification because some proprietors, as a result of their business experiences, may shift from one category to another. Nevertheless, it is useful for describing different patterns of female proprietorship and highlights the inadequacy of discussions which assume there is but one type of businesswoman. In this chapter, then, we review the more striking contrasts between innovative, conventional, radical and domestic proprietors and assess the degree to which in the 1980s and 1990s business ownership may enable some women to overcome experiences of gender disadvantage.

As we have already stated, conventional businesswomen are probably more numerous than any of the others. This is largely because they tend to create ventures in those sectors of economy where, for example, there are high concentrations of women employees and, often, women managers (see Chapter 2). Thus, many of these businesswomen have acquired some of the necessary trading and technical skills for start-up because of their earlier experiences as employees. Indeed, as long as a high proportion of women employees are confined to various unskilled retail, clerical and service occupations, there will continue to be the start-up of, for example, women-owned secretarial agencies, guest houses, fashion boutiques, hairdressing salons and office-cleaning businesses. Although, in common with the greater majority of both businessmen and women, the quest for personal autonomy is an important motive for start-up, the major driving force for these women is the need to acquire earnings in a manner compatible with their domestic obligations. How far, then, does this form of proprietorship enable them to overcome their subordination? Our evidence suggests hardly at all for three major reasons. First, most conventional entrepreneurs are married with children at the time of start-up, with the effect that their businesses are merely attached to a set of family relationships which many feminists regard as the major source of women's subordination. As such, their businesses are regarded as supplementary sources of income for meeting different family needs. Secondly, conventional business ownership rarely leads to a fundamental restructuring of conjugal roles. Women tend to retain their domestic duties despite their business responsibilities, and the help which they receive from their husbands in either sphere is highly limited. Consequently, any gains that proprietorship offers for personal working autonomy must be offset against the excessive demands and tensions which result from the need to balance business with family commitments. Thirdly, conventional businesswomen, who are often trading in those sectors where female employees are concentrated, help to preserve prevailing notions that certain occupational pursuits can be legitimately regarded as women's work. Indeed, as employers, they often rely heavily on relatively cheap and disposable part-time women workers and thereby sustain the secondary labour-market position of most female employees. Whilst, then, a small number of successful conventional businesswomen may expand their enterprises to the extent that these can no longer be regarded as secondary and additional to their domestic roles and a further small minority may become politically radicalized by their business experiences of male prejudice, the majority maintain their ventures within a set of personal relationships which reinforces rather than challenges their own and other women's subordination.

In a similar fashion to conventional businesswomen, domestic traders also tend to engage in activities which are traditionally regarded as women's work. In our study these included, for example, dressmakers, pottery producers, flower arrangers, china repairers and interior furnishers. However, their motivations for start-up differ significantly from those of the conventional proprietors. Economic needs, for instance, are not a primary consideration because, in most cases, domestic traders are married to managerial and professional employees whose salaries allow a relatively comfortable middle-class standard of living. Instead, the search for self-fulfilment and personal expression are paramount to the extent that they frequently regard their work as a craft or hobby rather than as a business pursuit. The practice of a craft, then, allows them to exercise creative skills and talents which would not otherwise be expressed within the domestic sphere. It also gives them a degree of personal autonomy, but this is always within the constraints stipulated by existing marriage and family relationships. Thus, although through trading such women are able to avoid total 'incorporation' into their husbands' careers and to develop more independent or 'non-vicarious' personal identities, their business activities rarely challenge the paramount priorities which they attach to the needs of their husbands and children. Indeed, many of them are aware of the potential risks should their businesses become too demanding and because of this they deliberately choose to restrict the scale of their trading activities. Of course, as long as they are married to husbands who earn relatively high salaries they can afford to forego business opportunities in the interests of other family members. Indeed, their dependence on the financial back-up and managerial skills of their husbands serves to encourage the view that, ultimately, their business activities are secondary to other family relationships.

Domestic traders, then, are frequently embedded within a set of relationships which sustains women's subordination. Their businesses give them opportunities for promoting their self-esteem and enable them to cope with, rather than to challenge, other facets of middle-class married life. However, the nature of their enterprises can be altered by the loss of their husbands' earnings. Sometimes this occurs because of divorce or marital break-up, but in other instances, it can happen through husbands becoming redundant or deciding to drop out of careers. In the latter circumstances, the wife's business can be drastically restructured in order to incorporate new needs. In particular, four changes in the nature of their businesses can be highlighted. First, it ceases to be a secondary activity and becomes the primary source of income. Secondly, it no longer functions as a separate and independent work sphere for wives; instead, husbands take a more active role in day-to-day trading activities. Thirdly, the business is organized on a more rational basis with a growing preoccupation with cash flow and trading profitability. Finally, such enterprises become geared to growth with greater attention devoted to market trends and potential business opportunities. In this process, domestic traders are transformed into co-proprietors of family businesses, but whether or not this better equips them to confront their subordination must remain an open question. On the one hand, it provides opportunities for the renegotiation of the domestic division of labour and a reassessment of the worth of women's work activities. But, on the other, it can allow husbands to take over overall business management and relegate their wives to subsidiary task-related roles which are compatible with existing domestic duties. In our view, the latter is more likely to occur; without management experience or business training, domestic traders are often ill-equipped to impose a more egalitarian partnership upon their husbands. Perhaps more importantly, few of them would want such a relationship; many of the women we interviewed regarded traditional gender roles as 'natural' and 'complementary'. In sum, domestic traders, either alone or in partnership with their husbands, are unlikely to seriously undermine the patriarchal nature of family relationships and the associated subordination of women, both within and beyond the domestic sphere.

By contrast, innovative entrepreneurs have explicitly rejected conventional gender relationships and are highly committed to personal achievement through business success. As we have pointed out, many will have encountered difficulties in their careers in large-scale organizations and they are determined to overcome these through business proprietorship. Indeed, it is their preoccupation with individual self-advancement through business growth which leads them to neglect all other interests. So much of their personal identity becomes locked into their businesses that there is little scope for personal and family relationships. Thus, in our study, only a minority of these women were married and even those with families gave overwhelming priority to their business interests. As such, they do manage to avoid the domestic subordination which is typically experienced by most domestic and conventional businesswomen. However, there are high personal costs which constrain any 'freedom' from subordination obtained through this route. Our evidence from the interviews supports this view in three ways. First, innovative entrepreneurs achieve their success through male-stipulated criteria of business and personal conduct. Many are quite prepared to emphasize their 'feminine charms' – as valued by men – if it helps them in their business interests. At the same time, they recognize the need to act 'tough' in a male fashion, recognizing their own lack of 'male aggression' as a major personal failing in the way they run their own enterprises. Secondly, and despite the differences which they acknowledge between men and women, they minimize the importance of gender as an influence upon individual life chances. In their view, women can best pursue their interests by personal effort, ability and self-help rather than by collective organization or by positive discriminatory measures by the state. For them, the majority of women fail not because of gender disadvantage but because they simply do not try hard enough. Finally, their almost total immersion in their businesses can alienate them in their personal lives from both men and women. As our interviews illustrate, they often become socially marginal with little in common with either women or men whose behaviour they are keen to emulate.

From a feminist perspective, then, innovative entrepreneurs do not change the system; they beat it by joining it. Their business success is won by adopting male values and by discarding their gender identity. In this process, they lose sympathy with the plight of other women and yet they are never fully accepted as equals by their male colleagues. Nevertheless, it is undeniable that these businesswomen achieve a level of material independence and personal autonomy which few other women are able to enjoy. Further, they experience a sense of self-fulfilment which they would rarely experience within the male-dominated world of employment. In the longer term, an increase in the number of these businesswomen may reduce the personal costs which they encounter, if only because of the greater availability of role models and an enhanced potential for networking and creating mutual support systems (Cooper, 1983). In view of the difficulties which many face in the pursuit of managerial careers, it is highly likely that increasing numbers of highly qualified women will turn to entrepreneurship as an alternative means for achieving material and personal success. [1] This may represent the most popular and successful individual strategy for combating gender subordination.

Radical proprietors, by contrast, regard their business activities as part of a collective struggle which offers services to other women in ways compatible with feminist ideology. They recognize the need for an ultimate and fundamental restructuring of society but, in the meantime, their businesses provide them with material support for the creation of identities and life-styles removed from the constraints of domestic subordination and patriarchal relationships. Radical businesswomen, in a similar fashion as innovative entrepreneurs, tend to be middle class in family background and often highly qualified, but they do not regard their expertise as a right to exclusive privileges; instead, it is a resource to be shared with other women. If they are successful as proprietors – that is, according to the conventional criterion of profitability – they obtain a material basis for the collective pursuit of feminist ideals. In this respect their business ventures offer a means for heightening the general level of feminist consciousness and for pursuing collective economic and social rights. Thus, there can be little doubt that of the various forms of business ownership we have considered, these are the only women to explicitly and forcefully challenge conventional gender relationships. Their co-owned and collectively organized enterprises provide spheres of autonomy which free them from male domination. However, despite this achievement there are reservations about their broader radical potential which need to be recognized. As Wajcman points out in a recent study of a working-class women's enterprise, co-operative organization does not, in itself, guarantee 'radical' or 'feminist' priorities. [2] As she states:

> the formation of a worker co-operative cannot simply be taken as an indication of radical political consciousness. Co-operatives are set up

for a number of reasons, ranging from ideological to more pragmatic ones, depending on the prevailing political circumstances and the consciousness and experience of the particular workers involved. Even within a single co-operative, the workers may have differing conceptions of it. The political impact of co-operatives is, then, an open question. (1983, p. 188)

Even the ability of relatively privileged middle-class women – of the sort we interviewed in our study – to confront their subordination through creating jointly owned business ventures can be severely constrained by their need to trade in a capitalist economy. For example, they often have to make swift business decisions which can undermine their commitment to collective consultation. Further, business growth can lead to hierarchy and impersonality which may challenge cherished ideals of egalitarianism and personal self-expression. Finally, trading success and the accumulation of profits can lead to dilemmas over the distribution of rewards and conflicts about the allocation of resources for new projects. Radical businesswomen, therefore, are constantly confronted with dilemmas stemming from ideals of sisterhood and the need to generate self-financing profits.

Despite these reservations the political potential of co-ownership ventures should not be underestimated (Gorz, 1982). The failure of the trade union movement in Britain to represent women's interests at work and its inability to combat class- and gender-based subordination is likely to encourage the growth of small-scale, self-help groups geared to trading for the purposes of material support. Further, the persistent strength of the women's movement and the numerical growth of highly educated and technically qualified women should provide the ideological and material conditions for the future expansion of radical forms of business ownership.

These, then, are some of the major observations derived from our interview survey. But what are the implications of these for the formulation of policies? There are two points to emphasize. First, although women share a number of common problems with men in business start-up and management, they do experience quite distinctive gender-related problems. Secondly, there are sharp contrasts among these women which policy-makers and small business advisors need to recognize. But, clearly, policies designed to encourage the formation and growth of women-owned businesses must operate at both general and specific levels.

At the general level all attempts to combat gender subordination, not just those directly associated with business proprietorship, can assist in the development of women-owned enterprises. In this sense, various equal-opportunity initiatives taken by employers, trade unions and the state can help women to obtain the necessary experience, knowledge and self-confidence for business start-up (Novarra, 1980; Davidson and Cooper, 1983a). Further, such changes can help to erode patterns of occupational segregation which restrict women's experience and, thus, their potential for proprietorship. But legislative reforms alone cannot create the necessary conditions for equal opportunity. Changes in workplace attitudes and practices will only be achieved if statutory measures are comprehensively backed up with programmes of education and training which are deliberately geared to combatting gender inequalities. Here the work of the Equal Opportunities Commission, the Manpower Services Commission, the Industrial Training Boards and, more recently, the European Economic Community's Social Fund can be of considerable importance (Cooper, ed., 1983).

Policies geared to the formation and growth of small businesses have, of course, increased over recent years (Beesley and Wilson, 1984). These have included new enterprise programmes, loan-guarantee schemes, tax and rate allowances and business-development grants. But, so far, the specific needs of businesswomen have been largely neglected (Watkins and Watkins, 1983). Indeed, there are no policies which recognize the particular problems which women face when they engage in start-up. In our view, there is a need for such policies. First, start-up courses which teach the basic techniques of bookkeeping, management and marketing need to be supplemented with methods for improving women's individual assertiveness, self-presentation and interpersonal negotiating skills (Smith *et al.*, 1984). These would be especially useful to aspiring businesswomen for their future dealings with employees and customers. Secondly, financial institutions need to be more generous in their offers of finance to women and more willing to ignore risk-avoiding 'track records' in commerce and trade. Often, they may have to waive for women their usual requirements for collateral and financial security. Finally, state agencies need to develop programmes of 'affirmative action', similar to those that operate in the United States, which ensure that a certain proportion of government contracts are allocated to business enterprises owned by women (Interagency Committee on Women's Business Enterprise, 1980). Without such forms of positive discrimination a large number of women will be unable to take advantage of small business opportunities during the coming decades.

However, it is important for small business policies to recognize that there are different types of businesswomen with striking contrasts in their needs. Compare, for example, the initial capital requirements of radical and domestic proprietors. Similarly, the interpersonal skills and managerial talents needed by these women are quite different. In our view, domestic traders are the least in need of assistance if only because they are relatively insulated from market forces and most protected by a well-established network of family and trading relationships. At the same time, they rarely recognize the need to improve women's opportunities in general, and it is unusual for them to trade solely for the purposes of economic self-gain. But as long as there is a demand for low-volume, high-quality specialist goods and services there will continue to be a niche in the market for these home-based, predominantly middle-class, domestic traders. Conventional businesswomen, by comparison, are in greater need of advice on how to manage their financial affairs as effectively as possible. They often trade in highly competitive markets where cash flows can be significantly improved with careful budgeting and planning. Even so, their domestic obligations normally restrict their commitment to business growth.

The real potential for the growth of small businesses is among those women whom we have described as innovators and radicals. As a result of their educational and occupational experiences, innovator proprietors are normally more aware of the available market opportunities. Moreover, their willingness to compromise with the male business world and to sacrifice personal and family relationships for the sake of their enterprises enables them to overcome many of the obstacles which many women face. Over the next decade, such women will be increasingly admired by the political right as the harbingers of a new economic order which values the qualities of individual effort, ambition, risk-taking and willpower. By contrast, the more radical proprietors will be encouraged by the political left, if only because they offer a means whereby limited feminist objectives can be attained within the context of de-industrialized economies. Such women are often highly aware of the different sources of funds and advice available for business start-up in addition to those from conventional banking; for example, the EEC Social Fund, the Co-operative Development Agency and the Greater London Enterprise Board are important potential sources of assistance. But they often need to acquire skills in developing appropriate legal forms of co-ownership and satisfactory techniques in such areas as break-even analysis, cash-flow projections and budgetary control.

Clearly, the development of women's businesses in the 1980s and 1990s will be shaped by a variety of economic, social and political forces. But it does seem certain that the flight from employment in large-scale organizations and the growth of smaller enterprises will continue as a result of structural economic changes and shifts in social and personal preferences. Both ends of the political spectrum in Britain now support this trend, although for totally contrasting ideological reasons. Thus, despite the persistence of large numbers of domestic and conventional businesswomen, proprietorship is most likely to expand among those we have described as radicals and innovators. In our view, both are concerned to overcome their experiences of subordination. But the means differ; whereas the former stress collectivism, the latter emphasize individualism. So, too, do they differ in their ends; innovators ultimately sustain the institutions of patriarchal capitalism, while radical proprietors seek to replace these with a socialist order within which all women will be able to enjoy a greater degree of self-determination. Until then, the appeal of business proprietorship will persist because it offers, if only to a variable and limited extent, a measure of autonomy which many women would otherwise be unable to enjoy.

Notes: Chapter 9

1 It can be argued that as organizational careers in the 1980s and 1990s become less predictable or long term, the opportunities for women increase relative to men because they cease to be disadvantaged by child-related career breaks. Equally, however, it can be suggested that as organizations contract the male claim to a diminishing supply of jobs may actually strengthen.

2 Wajcman (1983) also expresses reservations about the ability of working-class women to manage and organize co-operatives given their limited occupational experience. In the manufacturing sector this argument has considerable strength; in the service sector, where most women proprietors are, opportunities to develop skills necessary for proprietorship are often greater. Indeed, the acquisition of these skills through work experience is frequently more important at start-up than access to capital.

Bibliography

Allen, S. (1983), 'Production and reproduction: the lives of women homeworkers', *Sociological Review*, vol. 31.

Amsden, A. H. (ed.) (1980), *The Economics of Women and Work* (Harmondsworth, Middx: Penguin).

Ashridge Management College (1980), *Employee Potential – Issues in the Development of Women* (London: Institute of Personnel Management).

Barron, K. D., and Norris, G. M. (1976), 'Sexual divisions and the dual labour market', in D. Barker and S. Allen (eds), *Dependence and Exploitation in Work and Marriage* (London: Longman).

Bartol, K. M. (1980), 'Female managers and quality of working life: the impact of sex-role stereotypes', *Journal of Occupational Behaviour*, vol. 1.

Bechhofer, F., Elliott, B., Rushforth, M., and Bland, R. (1974a), 'The petits bourgeois in the class structure: the case of the small shopkeepers', in F. Parkin (ed.), *The Social Analysis of Class Structure* (London: Tavistock).

Bechhofer, F., Elliott, B., Rushforth, M., and Bland, R. (1974b), 'Small shopkeepers: matters of money and meaning', *Sociological Review*, vol. 22.

Beechey, V. (1982), 'Some notes on female wage labour in capitalist production', in M. Evans (ed.), *The Woman Question* (London: Fontana).

Beesley, M., and Wilson, P. (1984), 'Public policy and small firms in Britain', in C. Levicki (ed.), *Small Business: Theory and Policy* (London: Croom Helm).

Boissevain, J. (1980), *Small Entrepreneurs in Changing Europe: Towards a Research Agenda* (Utrecht: European Centre for Work and Society).

Braverman, H. (1974), *Labor and Monopoly Capital* (New York: Monthly Review Press).

Brown, R. (1976), 'Women as employees: some comments on research in industrial sociology', in D. Barker and S. Allen (eds), *Dependence and Exploitation in Work and Marriage* (London: Longman).

Brown, R. K., Brannen, P., Cousins, J. M., and Samphier, M. L. (1972), 'The contours of solidarity – social stratification and industrial relations in shipbuilding', *British Journal of Industrial Relations*, vol. 10.

Bruegel, I. (1982), 'Women as a reserve army of labour: a note on recent British experience', in M. Evans (ed.), *The Woman Question* (London: Fontana).

Burns, T. (ed.) (1969), *Industrial Man* (Harmondsworth, Middx: Penguin).

Cannon, I. C. (1967), 'Ideology and occupational community: a study of compositors', *Sociology*, vol. 1.

Caplan, P. (ed.) (1978), *Women United, Women Divided: Cross-Cultural Perspectives on Female Solidarity* (London: Fontana).

Carden, M. L. (1974), *The New Feminist Movement* (New York: Russell Sage).

Cavendish, R. (1982), *On the Line* (London: Routledge and Kegan Paul).

Central Office of Information (1975), *Women in Britain* (London: HMSO).

Central Statistical Office (1974), *Social Trends* (London: HMSO).

Clarke, J. (1979), 'Capital and culture: the post-war working class revisited', in J. Clarke, C. Critcher and R. Johnson (eds), *Working-Class Culture* (London: Hutchinson).

Cockburn, C. (1983), *Brothers: Male Dominance and Technological Change* (London: Pluto).

Committee of Inquiry on Small Firms (1971), *Report* (Bolton Report), Cmnd 4811 (London: HMSO).

Conservative Central Office (1979), *Small Business, Big Future* (London: Conservative Central Office).

Cooper, C. (1982), *Executive Families under Stress* (Englewood Cliffs, NJ: Prentice-Hall).

Cooper, C. (ed.) (1983), *Practical Approaches to Women's Career Development* (Sheffield: Manpower Services Commission).

Cooper, C., and Davidson, M. (1982), *High Pressure* (London: Fontana).

Coyle, A. (1984), *Redundant Women* (London: Women's Press).

Cragg, A., and Dawson, T. (1981), *Qualitative Research Among Homeworkers, Research Paper No. 21* (London: Department of Employment).

Davidson, M., and Cooper, C. (1983a), *Women Managers: Their Problems and What Can Be Done To Help Them* (Sheffield: Manpower Services Commission).

Davidson, M., and Cooper, C. (1983b), *Stress and the Woman Manager* (Oxford: Martin Robertson).

Day, G. (1982), 'Introduction', in G. Day (ed.), *Diversity and Decomposition in the Labour Market* (Aldershot, Hants: Gower).

Delamont, S. (1980), *The Sociology of Women* (London: Allen & Unwin).

Dennis, N., Henriques, F., and Slaughter, C. (1969), *Coal is Our Life* (London: Tavistock).

Department of Employment (1975a), *Women and Work: A Review*, Manpower Paper No. 10 (London: HMSO).

Department of Employment (1975b), *Women and Work: Overseas Practice*, Manpower Paper No. 12 (London: HMSO).

Department of Employment (1982), *New Earnings Survey 1981* (Part E) (London: HMSO).

Doeringer, P., and Piore, M. (1971), *Internal Labour Markets and Manpower Analysis* (Lexington, Mass.: D. C. Heath).

Dunnell, K. (1979), *Family Formation* (London: Office of Population Censuses and Surveys, HMSO).

Edgell, S. (1980), *Middle-Class Couples* (London: Allen & Unwin).

Epstein, C. F., and Coser, R. L. (1980), *Access to Power* (London: Allen & Unwin).

Eurostat (1981), *Economic and Social Position of Women in the Community* (Luxembourg: European Economic Community).

Evans, M. (ed.) (1982), *The Woman Question* (London: Fontana).

Finch, J. (1983), *Married to the Job* (London: Allen & Unwin).

Fogarty, M., Allen, I., and Walters, P. (1981), *Women in Top Jobs: 1968–1979* (London: HEB).

Fox, A. (1971), *A Sociology of Work in Industry* (London: Collier Macmillan).

Fox, A. (1974), *Beyond Contract: Work, Power and Trust Relations* (London: Faber).

Gershuny, J. (1978), *After Industrial Society* (London: Macmillan).

Giddens, A. (1973), *The Class Structure of the Advanced Societies* (London: Hutchinson).

Goffee, R., and Scase, R. (1982a), 'Fraternalism and paternalism as employer strategies in small firms', in G. Day (ed.), *Diversity and Decomposition in the Labour Market* (Aldershot, Hants: Gower).

Goffee, R., and Scase, R. (1982b), 'Female entrepreneurs: some preliminary research findings', *Service Industries Review*, vol. 2.

Goffee, R., and Scase, R. (1983a), 'Business ownership and women's subordination: a preliminary study of female proprietors', *Sociological Review*, vol. 31.

Goffee, R., and Scase, R. (1983b), 'Class, entrepreneurship and the service sector: towards a conceptual classification', *Service Industries Journal*, vol. 3.

Goffee, R., and Scase, R. (1983c). *Female Proprietors and the Role of Women in Small-Scale Capital Accumulation*, Euromed Working Paper No. 34 (Amsterdam: University of Amsterdam).

Goffee, R., and Scase, R. (1984), 'Proprietorial control in family firms: some functions of quasi-organic management systems', *Journal of Management Studies*, vol. 21.

Goffee, R., Scase, R., and Pollack, M. (1981), 'Letter from America to business persons', *Guardian*, 2 October.

Goffee, R., Scase, R., and Pollack, M. (1982), 'Why some women decide to become their own boss', *New Society*, 9 September.

Goldthorpe, J. H., with Llewellyn, C., and Payne, C. (1980), *Social Mobility and Class Structure in Modern Britain* (Oxford: Clarendon Press).

Goldthorpe, J. H., Lockwood, D., Bechhofer, F., and Platt, J. (1968), *The Affluent Worker: Industrial Attitudes and Behaviour* (Cambridge: University Press).

Gorb, P. (1981), *Small Business Perspectives* (London: Armstrong Publishing).

Gordon, D. (1972), *Theories of Poverty and Underemployment* (Lexington, Mass.: D. C. Heath).

Gorz, A. (1982), *Farewell to the Working Class: An Essay on Post-Industrial Socialism* (London: Pluto Press).

Gould, M. (1979), 'When women create an organisation: the ideological imperatives of feminism', in D. Dunkerley and G. Salaman (eds), *The International Yearbook of Organisation Studies* (London: Routledge & Kegan Paul).

Hakim, C. (1979), *Occupational Segregation*, Research Paper No. 9 (London: Department of Employment).

Hakim, C. (1981), 'Job segregation: trends in the 1970s', *Employment Gazette*.

Handy, C. (1984), *The Future of Work* (Oxford: Blackwell).

Heath, A. (1981), *Social Mobility* (London: Fontana).

Hennig, M., and Jardim, A. (1979), *The Managerial Woman* (London: Pan).

Herzog, M. (1980), *From Hand to Mouth* (Harmondsworth, Middx: Penguin).

Hunt, A. (1975), *Management Attitudes and Practices Towards Women at Work* (London: Office of Population Censuses and Surveys, HMSO).

Hunt, J. (1982), 'A woman's place is in her union', in J. West (ed.), *Work, Women and the Labour Market* (London: Routledge & Kegan Paul).

Hurstfield, J. (1978), *The Part-Time Trap* (London: Low Pay Unit).

Interagency Task Force on Women Business Owners (1978), *The Bottom Line: Unequal Enterprise in America* (Washington DC. United States Government Printing Office).

Interagency Committee on Women's Business Enterprise (1980), *Annual Report to the President 1980* (Washington DC: United States Government Printing Office).

Joseph, G. (1983), *Women at Work* (Oxford: Philip Allen).

Kanter, R. M. (1977), *Men and Women of the Corporation* (New York: Basic Books).

Kanter, R. M. (1981), 'Women and the structure of organisations: explorations in theory and behaviour', in O. Grunsky and G. A. Miller (eds), *The Sociology of Organisations*, 2nd edn. (New York: Free Press).

Kets de Vries, M. F. R. (1977), 'The entrepreneurial personality: a person at the crossroads', *Journal of Management Studies*, vol. 14.

Kinzer, N. S. (1980), *Stress and the American Woman* (New York: Ballantyne Books).

Korn Ferry International (1982), *Profile of Women Senior Executives* (New York: Korn Ferry).

Kornhauser, A. (1960), *The Politics of Mass Society* (London: Routledge & Kegan Paul).

Larwood, L., and Wood, M. M. (1977), *Women in Management* (London: Lexington Books).

Leighton, P. (1983), *Contractual Arrangements In Selected Industries*, Research Paper No. 39 (London: Department of Employment).

Light, I. (1972), *Ethnic Enterprise in America* (Berkeley, Calif.: University of California Press).

McClelland, D. (1961), *The Achieving Society* (Princetown, NJ: Van Nostrand).

MacKenzie, G. (1973), *The Aristocracy of Labour* (Cambridge: Cambridge University Press).

Mackie, L., and Patullo, P. (1977), *Women at Work* (London: Tavistock).

McNally, F. (1979), *Women for Hire* (London: Macmillan).

Mann, M. (1973), *Consciousness and Action among the Western Working Class* (London: Macmillan).

Manpower Report (1977) 'The changing economic role of women', in N. Glazer and H. Youngelson Waehrer (eds), *Woman in a Man-made World*, 2nd edn. (Chicago: Rand McNally).

Martin, J., and Roberts, C. (1984), *Women and Employment: A Lifetime Perspective* (London: Department of Employment and Office of Population Censuses and Surveys: HMSO).

Mednik, M., Tangri, S., and Hoffman, L. (eds) (1975), *Women and Achievement* (Washington DC: Hemisphere).

Miller, D. C., and Form, W. H. (1964), *Industrial Sociology* (New York: Harper & Row).

Mills, C. W. (1953), *White Collar* (New York: Oxford University Press).

Mitchell, J. (1971), *Women's Estate* (Harmondsworth, Middx: Penguin).

Morgan, R. (1970), 'Introduction: the women's revolution', in R. Morgan (ed.), *Sisterhood Is Powerful* (New York: Vintage Books).

Nelson, L. (1978), 'Women must help each other: female beer producers in

Kenya', in P. Caplan (ed.), *Women United, Women Divided: Cross-Cultural Perspectives on Female Solidarity* (London: Fontana).

Newby, H. (1977), 'Paternalism and capitalism', in R. Scase (ed.), *Industrial Society: Class, Cleavage and Control* (London: Allen & Unwin).

Newby, H., Bell, C., Rose, D., and Saunders, P. (1978), *Property, Paternalism and Power* (London: Hutchinson).

Novarra, V. (1980), *Women's Work, Men's Work* (London: Marion Boyars).

Oakley, A. (1982), *Subject Women* (London: Fontana).

Office of Population Censuses and Surveys (1981), *Labour Force Survey 1981* (London: HMSO).

Oppenheimer, V. (1970), *The Female Labour Force in the United States* (Berkeley, Calif.: University of California Press).

Pahl, J. M., and Pahl, R. E. (1972), *Managers and their Wives* (Harmondsworth, Middx: Penguin).

Pahl, R. E. (1980), 'Employment, work and the domestic division of labour', *International Journal of Urban and Regional Research*, vol. 4.

Parkin, F. (1971), *Class Inequality and Political Order* (London: Macgibbon & Kee).

Peters, T., and Waterman, R. (1982), *In Search of Excellence* (New York: Harper & Row).

Place, H. (1979), 'A biographical profile of women in management', *Journal of Occupational Psychology*, vol. 52.

Pollert, A. (1981), *Girls, Wives, Factory Lives* (London: Macmillan).

Purcell, K. (1979), 'Militancy and acquiescence amongst women workers', in S. Burman (ed.), *Fit Work for Women* (London: Croom Helm).

Rapoport, R., and Rapoport, R. (1976), *Dual Career Families Re-examined* (Oxford: Martin Robertson).

Reid, I. (1982), 'Vital statistics', in I. Reid and E. Wormald (eds), *Sex Differences in Britain* (London: Grant McIntyre).

Reid, I., and Wormald, E. (eds) (1982), *Sex Differences in Britain* (London: Grant McIntyre).

Roethlisberger, F. J., and Dickson, W. J. (1939), *Management and the Worker* (Cambridge, Mass.: Harvard University Press).

Royal Commission on Income Distribution and Wealth (1979), *Report No. 8* (London: HMSO).

Runciman, W. G. (1966), *Relative Deprivation and Social Justice* (London: Routledge & Kegan Paul).

Salaman, G. (1979), *Work Organisations* (London: Longman).

Sanders, D., and Reid, J. (1982), *Kitchen Sink or Swim: Women in the Eighties* (Harmondsworth, Middx: Penguin).

Scase, R., and Goffee, R. (1980a), *The Real World of the Small Business Owner* (London: Croom Helm).

Scase, R., and Goffee, R. (1980b), 'Home life in a small business', *New Society*, 30 October.

Scase, R., and Goffee, R. (1981), 'Traditional petty bourgeois attitudes: the case of the self-employed craftsman', *Sociological Review*, vol. 29.

Scase, R., and Goffee, R. (1982), *The Entrepreneurial Middle Class* (London: Croom Helm).

Scase, R., and Goffee, R. (1983), 'The small businessman as an employer', *Social Science Research Council Newsletter 49*, June.

Sebastyen, A. (1979), 'Tendencies in the movement: then and now', in *Feminist Practice: Notes from the Tenth Year* (London: In Theory Press).

Silverstone, R., and Ward, A. (eds) (1980), *Careers of Professional Women* (London: Croom Helm).

Sinfield, A. (1981), *What Unemployment Means* (Oxford: Martin Robertson).

Smith, M., *et al.* (1984), *A Development Programme for Women in Management* (Aldershot, Hants: Gower Press).

Stanworth, J., and Curran, J. (1973), *Management Motivation in the Smaller Business* (Aldershot, Hants: Gower Press).

Stanworth, M. (1984), 'Women and class analysis: a reply to Goldthorpe', *Sociology*, vol. 18.

Storey, D. J., (1982), *Entrepreneurship and the New Firm* (London: Croom Helm).

Swedish Institute (1980), *Fact Sheet on Sweden No. 260* (London).

United States Department of Commerce (1980), *Selected Characteristics of Women-owned Businesses 1977* (Washington DC: Bureau of the Census).

United States Small Business Administration (1983), *The State of Small Business: A Report of the President* (Washington DC: US Government Printing Office).

United States Small Business Administration (1982), *Fact Sheet No. 45* (Office of Public Communications, March).

Vanek, J. (ed.) (1975), *Self-Management* (Harmondsworth, Middx: Penguin).

Wainright, H. (1978), 'Women and the division of labour', in P. Abrams (ed.), *Work, Urbanism and Inequality: UK Society Today* (London: Weidenfeld & Nicolson).

Wajcman, J. (1983), *Women in Control* (Milton Keynes, Bucks: Open University).

Watkins, J., and Watkins, D. (1983), *Training Needs and the Female Entrepreneur*, Paper presented to 6th Annual UK Small Business Conference, Durham (1–3 September).

Webb, M. (1982), 'The labour market', I. Reid and E. Wormald (eds), in *Sex Differences in Britain* (London: Grant McIntyre).

West, J. (1982), 'Introduction', in J. West (ed.) *Work, Women and the Labour Market* (London: Routledge & Kegan Paul).

West, J. (ed.) (1982), *Work, Women and the Labour Market* (London: Routledge & Kegan Paul).

Westergaard J., and Resler, H. (1976), *Class in a Capitalist Society* (Harmondsworth, Middx: Penguin).

Wilkin, M. (1982), 'Educational opportunity and achievement', in I. Reid and E. Wormald (eds), *Sex Differences in Britain* (London: Grant McIntyre).

Wright, D. H. (1979), *Co-operatives and Community: The Theory and Practice of Producer Co-operatives* (London: Bedford Square Press).

Index